PEACE ON EARTH

PEACE ON EARTH

A Commentary on Pope John's Encyclical

PETER RIGA

HERDER AND HERDER

1964
HERDER AND HERDER   NEW YORK
232 Madison Avenue, New York 16, N. Y.

Library of Congress Catalog Card Number 64–13691
© 1964 by Herder and Herder, Incorporated
Printed in the United States of America

DILECTISSIMAE · MEMORIAE
HUMILLIME · DEDICAVIT
PAPAE · JOANNIS · XXIII
QUEM · FORTISSIME · AMAVIT
AUCTOR

CONTENTS

PEACE ON EARTH

Foreword

THIS papal document is unprecedented in history.[1] It is addressed not only to the five-hundred-million members of the Church whose beloved shepherd is the successor of St. Peter, but it is framed as an "open letter to the whole world," as a dialogue with all men of good will. It has been greeted with unanimous acclaim by the press of the whole world, and has aroused responsive echoes among all the nations of the earth. It speaks in a language that is simple, direct, and man-to-man. It was born of a great trust in God and at the same time of a trust in man, in that which is best in him.

One writer has compared it with Beethoven's Ninth Symphony, and has called it "the symphony of peace." It has a fundamental theme, four movements, and a finale. The theme which recurs, like a leitmotif, nine times, and which is especially developed in the third part of the encyclical, is in these words: "Peace among all peoples requires: Truth as its foundation, justice as its rule, love as its driving force, liberty as its atmosphere." This theme underlies each of the four sections that correspond to the four movements of the symphony and that fix the major laws which govern it: Peace in the harmony of individuals with each other; peace in the harmony between individuals and their political communities; peace in the harmony between political communities; peace in the harmony between individuals and political groups on the one hand and the whole community of men on the other.

[1]Statement by Léon-Joseph Cardinal Suenens, made on May 13, 1963, at the annual Conference on Non-Governmental Organizations of the United Nations, reprinted here by special permission of His Eminence.

I should like to focus with you on certain central ideas which are like peaks in a range of mountains that form the summit line which dominates the surroundings and keep them in proportion. This focusing on the essentials is made easier by the fact that the pope has gone straight to the heart of the matter without detours or circumlocutions but simply with an outburst of his heart. The Holy Father recently said to me: "There are people who like to make simple things complicated. I like to make complicated things simple." The encyclical is a striking illustration of those words. It is simple, but it has a simplicity which is the exact opposite of facile simplifications. It does not ignore the complexities of the problems that have to be met or the antagonisms that have to be reconciled. It does not ignore the burden of history. But over and above those things that divide us, it focuses on those that unite us. A statesman once said:

I think that there exists among men—more often than we think—a common denominator. It is like a blackboard. You write a whole lot of big complicated fractions that seem irreconcilable and you know that by various arithmetical operations, by various successive eliminations, you can finally reach their common denominator, which is a very simple little figure that you never could have foreseen from the thickets.

That is what the encyclical "Peace on Earth" is. It is the discovery of the common denominator among men of good will. Once that is understood, it remains only for us to make—not an analysis, for it is too abundant—but only a rapid examination. It seems to me that in the encyclical we can discern a fourfold appeal: An appeal for respect for the individual; an appeal for collaboration among nations; an appeal for the creation of a supranational power; an appeal for collaboration among men

12

despite their ideological differences. Let us examine each of these, one by one.

1. *Appeal for respect for the individual.* At the start of this mountain range there stands, like a Mont Blanc dominating the terrain, the basic affirmation of the inviolable and inalienable rights of each individual human being. Any dialogue among men is impossible unless all sides accept a hierarchy of values or at least a first principle which governs everything. That principle, the encyclical tells us, is the recognition of the dignity and rights of the individual. At the start, the pope connects the dialogue with delegates of the United Nations who promulgated, on December 10, 1948, the Universal Declaration of the Rights of Man. That declaration solemnly recognizes for all men without exception their individual dignity. It affirms for every individual his rights to seek freely for truth, to follow the rules of morality, to practice the duties of justice, to demand living conditions that conform to human dignity. Those inalienable and sacred rights the pope reaffirms, sets forth in detail, and defines. Those rights, he declares, are valid and necessary in all latitudes and longitudes, without regard to place, or to racial, political, ideological or religious differences. Respect for those rights is at the foundation of every social structure. A well-known author (St.-Exupéry) put this thought very well when he said: "If respect for man is established in the hearts of men, men will succeed by establishing in return a social, political, and economic system that will enshrine that respect."

But if the respect due to the individual is the starting point for every civilization, it is to the individual that we must return to begin the movement of opening up to others which, step by step, will bring about the peace of the world. This opening up to

13

others, far from contradicting the true personality of man, is an integrating factor. A person who turns inward, who turns away from society, weakens, stifles, and ultimately denies himself. The relationship to others is located as of right in the heart of the true personality and assists its development. It is therefore in the souls of each one of us and at the outset that the peace of the world is cast. It is from there that it must spread out, in concentric circles, to the limits of the universe. It is from there that it must extend, more and more, like waves which carry images and which need successive relay stations to go around the world. International peace begins in the souls of each one of us. Its boundary line is not marked by this or that river or ocean or mountain range. It coincides, at the start, with the frontiers of our hearts. Peace must begin at this first level, if we wish to erect, stone by stone, the vast and complex edifice of peace among nations.

Peace begins at home. Charity begins at home—according to the saying that you know so well—but I hasten to add: Charity must not remain at home. Peace begins in the bosom of each family, and spreads from there to the street, to the neighborhood, to the city, to the nation, to the world. Each gesture of peace, each little peace, each small-scale decision, helps the big-scale decisions that carry into effect peace among nations. General peace depends upon peace in these particular situations, these humble and modest efforts at pacification which are being accomplished without fanfare, in all social classes and at all levels. The father who settles a family dispute and brings his household together, the office worker who settles a quarrel and changes the atmosphere of his surroundings, the employer and the union leader who make an effort to understand each other and overcome the antagonisms between their particular interests, the history professor who lights up the past with serene objectivity—all these, and I could go on indefinitely—bring their own precious contributions to the building of peace. If we are not to lose all reality, we must never neglect any work of peace that is within our reach.

2. *Appeal for collaboration among nations.* But individuals are not isolated. They are parts of political communities. "These political communities," the encyclical tells us, "must harmonize their relations according to truth and justice, in the spirit of active solidarity and in liberty." *Truth* requires us to recognize "the natural equality of all political communities in dignity and human nobility." Truth requires us to treat every people with serene objectivity. Truth requires us to eliminate all news-disseminating procedures that do unjust harm to the reputation to any people. *Justice* in turn implies recognition "of mutual rights and the fulfillment of their corresponding duties." Justice requires that "when political communities advance opposing interests, the conflicts may be settled neither by force of arms nor by fraud or deceit, but by mutual understanding, by an objective appraisal of the facts and by an equitable compromise." *The sense of solidarity* requires that peoples do not close themselves off in narrow compartments and that they place in common their individual riches, at all levels, and that they enter into broad mutual interchanges. The sense of liberty finally demands abstention from intrusion into the internal affairs of other peoples and the encouraging in others of the development of the sense of responsibility and of initiative. Such, briefly, are the rules of the road which lead to peace, rules which must be respected in the relations between the various political communities.

This fundamental principle of necessary collaboration between people collides, as you know, with that drama of our century which is called the armaments race. If we want the nations to build together the peace of the world, we must as soon as possible free the way and escape from this impasse. Thus the solemn warning on disarmament that the Pope addresses to the world:

On the other hand, it is with deep sorrow that We note the enormous stocks of armaments that have been and still are being made in more economically developed countries, with a vast outlay of intellectual and economic resources. And so it happens that while the people of these countries are loaded with heavy burdens, other countries as a result are deprived of the collaboration they need in order to make economic and social progress.

The production of arms is allegedly justified on the grounds that in present-day conditions peace cannot be preserved without an equal balance of armaments. And so, if one country increases its armaments, others feel the need to do the same; and if one country is equipped with nuclear weapons, other countries must produce their own, equally destructive.

Consequently, people live in constant fear lest the storm that every moment threatens should break upon them with dreadful violence. And with good reason, for the arms of war are ready at hand. Even though it is difficult to believe that anyone would deliberately take the responsibility for the appalling destruction and sorrow that war would bring in its train, it cannot be denied that the conflagration may be set off by some uncontrollable and unexpected chance. And one must bear in mind that even though the monstrous power of modern weapons acts as a deterrent, it is to be feared that the mere continuance of nuclear tests, undertaken with war in mind, will have fatal consequences for life on the earth.

Justice, then, right reason, and humanity urgently demand that the arms race should cease; that the stockpiles which exist in various countries should be reduced equally and simultaneously by the parties concerned; that nuclear weapons should be banned; and that finally a general agreement should be reached about progressive disarmament and an effective method of control.

This is an appeal for reconciliation, for a dialogue between peoples. Confidence cannot be born overnight; but between blind confidence and systematic distrust, there is room for a measured and progressive trust. A journey of a thousand leagues, according to an Oriental proverb, begins with a single step. The Sovereign Pontiff invites the peoples to progress toward trust, toward an opening to others not only personal but collective. But if the path is long and arduous it merits being followed. This effort is "both demanded by reason, supremely desirable and of the greatest usefulness." The people do not have a choice: either they choose the armaments race with, as the end of this rivalry, the permanent risk of collective nuclear suicide; or they select the progressive trust which alone can engender the trust necessary to the stability of the peace.

But this is only the elimination of an obstacle. A true collaboration between peoples demands a positive converging effort. If the nightmare of the armaments race disappears from the horizon, almost unlimited possibilities of fruitful collaboration will present themselves. We can then begin to solve, by indispensable and urgent collaboration, according to the scale of our needs, the principal social problem of our time. This problem, as we all know, is that of the developing countries. No man of good will can accept the fact that two-thirds of the world—two million of every three million men—do not attain the level of normal human development that technology places at the disposition of privileged peoples. No one can accept coldly the fact that two men out of every three live in an undernourished state. No one can accept such a flagrant inequality of the distribution of the fruits of the earth. Civilization is not worthy of its name if it resigns itself to this collective social sin.

This disproportion, this disequilibrium, hangs with all its weight on the peace of the world, but, even if this were not the case, no one could accept passively this situation of collective social injustice, the most flagrant of our century. It is necessary to break, at any price, the vicious circle which results in men being poor throughout the greater part of the world because they produce too little and produce too little because they are too poor to produce more. It is necessary to attack the evil at its roots and bring all our powers to bear so that every individual and every people can attain the level of human dignity, the "level of hope" in a better future. Time is short.

In a world which counts an additional man every second, one has not the right to be an hour behind. Misery does not wait.

Two out of every three men suffer from an endemic of acute hunger. Every year, of sixty million deaths, hunger and its consequences cause thirty to forty million, that is to say as much as the last war, in five years, with all its resources and destruction.

It is necessary that this "unmerited misery" of peoples cease. Another reason that "the swords," of which the Prophet Isaias spoke, become "plowshares."

The hour has come for a vast collective movement of aid and of effective solidarity at the scale of our needs.

But in order that this aid may be valid and accepted, the encyclical asserts an essential condition: "That this indispensable aid be given with full respect for the *liberty* of the developing peoples."

It does not suffice to wish good *for* someone. It is necessary to wish it *with* him, with respect for his own personality, with the fundamental concern of aiding him to become himself and to reveal himself to himself and to the world. The necessary aid ought be granted always in the framework of these words of the

French philosopher, Louis Lavelle: "The greatest good that we can do to others is not to transmit our riches to them, but to discover theirs." The pope expressed this same concern with these words: "Let us underline it with emphasis, the aid brought to these people cannot be accompanied by any fetters on their independence. They must besides feel themselves principally responsible for their economic and social progress." These words echo the invitation formulated already in another encyclical *Mater et Magistra.* This document, devoted to economic and social problems, completes the thought of *Pacem in terris* in these words:

Economically developed states must take the greatest care so that in coming to aid the developing countries they do not seek their own political advantage in a spirit of domination.

If that is going to happen it will be necessary to declare firmly that it is not to establish a colonization of a new type, masked, without a doubt, but no less dominating than that which numerous political communities have recently left. This would damage international relations and create a danger for the peace of the world.

It is indispensable therefore and justice requires that this technical and financial aid be transmitted in the most sincere political disinterestedness. It must have the objective of placing the communities in the path of economic development and at the same time of realizing by their own efforts their economic and social progress.

In order to act effectively, with regard to the extent of the problem to be resolved and its complexity, men must believe with a strong conviction that the solution is realizable and that it is within reach of their efforts.

At the time of the United States War of Secession, Admiral Dupont laboriously explained to Admiral Farragut one day why he could not bring his warships into the port at Charleston. Farragut, after having heard him out, said:

"Dupont, there is one more reason."

"What then?"

"You did not *believe* that you could do it."

In order to achieve the progress of the developing countries, we must *believe* that this work does not exceed our combined forces. Where there is a will, there is a way. The Sovereign Pontiff asks men of good will to believe in the possibilities of succeeding in this most extensive work which is worthy of man and of his most noble aspirations.

3. *Appeal for the creation of a supranational power.* In order to be effective and real this collaboration among peoples requires, at the highest level, a coordinating organ. This is why His Holiness John XXIII concluded his exhortation for collaboration by all with an appeal for a better organization of the public powers charged with assuring the universal common good. The extent of these problems to be resolved is, of itself, an invitation to constitute a public authority of worldwide scope, it being always understood that the principle of "subsidiarity" must control the relations of this world authority with the governments of states and that the latter retain, within their own sphere, the exercise of their responsibilities. The pope writes:

Today the universal common good poses problems of worldwide dimensions which cannot be adequately tackled or solved except by the efforts of public authorities endowed with a wideness of powers, structure, and means of the same proportions, that is, of public authorities which are in a position to operate in an effective manner on a worldwide basis. The moral order itself, therefore, demands that such a form of public authority be established.

And the pope continues:

A public authority having worldwide power and endowed with the proper means for the efficacious pursuit of its objective, which is the universal common good in concrete form, must be set up by common accord and not imposed by force. The reason is that such an authority must be in a position to operate effectively; yet at the same time its action must be inspired by sincere and real impartiality. In other words, it must be an action aimed at satisfying the objective requirements of the universal common good. The difficulty is that there would be reason to fear that a supranational or worldwide public authority, imposed by force by the more powerful political communities, might be or might become an instrument of one-sided interests; and even should this not happen, it would be difficult for it to avoid all suspicion of partiality in its actions, and this would take away from the efficaciousness of its activity. Even though there may be pronounced differences between political communities as regards the degree of their economic development and their military power, they are all very sensitive as regards their juridical equality and their moral dignity. For that reason they are right in not easily yielding in obedience to an authority imposed by force, or to an authority in whose creation they had no part, or to which they themselves did not decide to submit by conscious and free choice.

And the pope concludes with this wish:

It is Our earnest wish that the United Nations Organization, in its structure and in its means, may become ever more equal to the magnitude and nobility of its tasks. May the day soon come when every human being will find therein an effective safeguard for the rights which derive directly from his dignity as a person and which are therefore universal, inviolate, and inalienable rights. This is all the more to be hoped for since all human beings, as they take an ever more active part in the public life of their own political communities, are showing an increasing interest in the affairs of all peoples, and are becoming more consciously aware that they are living members of the universal family of mankind.

4. *Appeal for collaboration among men despite their ideological differences*. The encyclical contains a fourth appeal: for collaboration among men in the economic, social and political domains despite ideologies which place them in opposition.

21

However, one must never confuse error and the person who errs. . . . It must be borne in mind, furthermore, that neither can false philosophical teachings regarding the nature, origin and destiny of the universe and of man, be identified with historical movements that have economic, social, cultural, or political ends, not even when these movements have originated from those teachings and have drawn and still draw inspiration therefrom. For these teachings, once they are drawn up and defined, remain always the same, while the movements, working on historical situations in constant evolution, cannot but be influenced by these latter and cannot avoid, therefore, being subject to changes, even of a profound nature.

That is to say that it is not necessary to identify the flesh and bone men with whom we come in contact according to the abstract logic of the ideologies that they profess. Every Christian knows that the Christianity which inspires him is worth more than the practical translation which he gives it because of weakness and egoism in his daily life. He must know that the opposite is also true: it happens that one may join and cooperate in social efforts emanating from those whose principles, for one reason or another, one cannot accept.

His Holiness John XXIII, at the conclusion of his letter, invites us to go forward to the discovery of men beyond the ideologies which oppose them to one another. And what is true for men is true for peoples. Neither can the latter be identified with the political systems in which they exist. A limitless field of discovery opens there before us. Today people are not more ignorant, but they do not know themselves further. A quarter of an hour passed in some airport shows to what degree men of five continents come together and are seized by the same rhythm of life. But this encounter is not yet a meeting. People are elbow to elbow, but each is lost in the anonymous crowd; no one has given his name nor shown his true visage. We are still far from the grouping together of people, farther yet from a real communion and from human friendship. Men pass, side by side, as hurried and distracted travelers without exchanging a word, nor a fraternal handshake nor a smile. We do not seek to know what constitutes the profound soul of each people. We do now know the hidden treasures of culture and of noble traditions which could become, in the interchange, a common good for humanity and an enrichment for all. A first revolution will be made if men learn simply to speak to each other and not only to co-exist side by side.

Our century has discovered interplanetary space, but it has hardly explored the space which separates men from each other. Our century has thrown gigantic bridges over rivers, but it does not yet know how to build bridges from people to people and to join the two sides. Our century has discovered nuclear energy, but it has yet to discover the creative energy of peace and of concord which embodies a simple act of love and of mutual understanding. It is for qualified and wise statesmen, the encyclical tells us, to determine the stages, the means, and the extent of reconciliation among peoples, but it is for each of us, starting now, to create the atmosphere therefor. The least effort of justice and of equity, of objectivity and of understanding in public relations opens the way toward this revolution to which humanity aspires and which looks toward the introduction and the stabilization of peace among men. In addressing to you, as a supreme testament, this charter on peace, His Holiness John XXIII has only one ambition and one desire: to render the earth a better place in which mankind may live.

LÉON–JOSEPH CARDINAL SUENENS

INTRODUCTION

No encyclical in modern times has received the universal and spontaneous acclaim that *Pacem in terris* has from every part of the world, from Protestant, Jewish, and non-Christian sources. The United States government, which normally ignores papal statements, strongly praised the document, and even the Communist press had words of approval. Such praise is not without foundation. *Pacem in terris* is undoubtedly one of the strongest and most eloquent papal statements on peace ever made. And since its firm basis is taken from political and moral philosophy, it could be addressed "to all men of good will." If peace is to come, it must be based on a moral as well as a political and constitutional recognition of the rights of every man on the face of the globe.

In his encyclical the late Holy Father stated clearly that there is a basic core of humanity which must be respected if peace is to be achieved. The Holy Father defined this core as the inviolable, inalienable, and universal rights of the human person; these are essential to a sane conception of any present or future national and international order. The function of any state is only to promote, protect, and facilitate the exercise of these rights. Thus, they are called civil rights only insofar as they are guaranteed in laws and constitutions. But fundamentally they belong to every human being—man or woman, black or white, rich or poor, strong or weak—by the very fact that he possesses human nature. These rights are not to be violated by government or by other individuals. Unless men incorporate this basic structure in declarations of human rights, international laws, and constitutions, men are simply wasting time and endangering true peace. To insure against this kind of error, Pope John XXIII consecrated the entire first part of *Pacem in terris* to a careful analysis of these rights. In a sense, then, this encyclical is a forceful justification of all the rights of the human person.

The two encyclicals *Mater et Magistra* and *Pacem in terris* form, as it were, two sides of the same coin. Man is both spirit and matter; this mysterious combination called man cannot be defined without these essential qualities. *Mater et Magistra* stresses the incarnational reality of man. To preach the supernatural to man is insufficient; God has created man as flesh and bone, and for man to live as God has willed him to live, he must live in economic dignity and justice. The order of creation and incarnation both demand this. And because he is created as a totality in the image and likeness of God, man is associated, in an essential fashion, with something of the divine: thus, every man who lives or ever will live is incomparably more valuable than the whole of the created cosmos. As a result, man has dignity simply because he comes from God's creating hands with dignity. The divine source of human dignity would not be contested by any Christian, Jew, or other theist. Even if disagreement arises in our pluralistic community over the source of this dignity, there are few in the free world who would dispute the reality. On that basis, there is much room for a common cause.

Thought is powerful because it clarifies false images and dispels outright lies; but it is proved by action. A common work for a common goal may enable all men of good will to appreciate and finally to love each other. Nothing can be accomplished without the driving force of love. In *Pacem in terris,* the great church-man and humanitarian, John XXIII, suggested as a common endeavor the promotion of what is most sacred in all men: human and civil rights and liberties. Here is a program in which the Jew, the Christian, and even the secularist can give of himself to other men to make his true image concrete—the image of a man who is not simply interested in promoting himself and his group (as has too often been the case in the past) but is sincerely and genu-inely interested in others, regardless of color, creed, national origin, or ethnic group. In reality, only in such a common en-deavor can men come to respect and ultimately to love each other.

John XXIII gave this encyclical on peace to the world, to all men of good will. This in itself is extraordinary; for the first time in the history of papal encyclicals, the entire world is addressed directly. It is an appeal for peace so firm in doctrine and so elo-quent in tone that it has already given pause to men of every ideology and in every walk of life. But no one must be deceived. The late Holy Father only epitomized what the holy Church has always maintained in her ordinary teaching: the common origin and dignity of man, his rights and duties, and the concept of authority in the promotion of these rights on both a national and an international level. But by embodying these Church teachings in the text of an encyclical, John XXIII gave them an intensity and emphasis not previously enjoyed.

The novelty of the encyclical is that Pope John presented the Church's teaching in a way which is in profound accord with modern aspirations—for international rights, disarmament, inde-pendence, the world community, economic and cultural dignity, and so on. The encyclical expresses these aspirations in the lan-guage of modern man. Pius XII had already said many of the things contained here, but for the first time, a document from the Holy See uses the modern vocabulary of the rights of man. In fact, it is the first time that a papal document has given so much attention and praise to a secular document such as the Universal Declaration of the Rights of Man.

This new way of announcing eternal truths marks a refreshing and important turn in the history of the Church. This mode of expression breaks with four and a half centuries of the Church's fearful distrust of modern man, brought on by the Renaissance and the Reformation. Pope John spoke directly to modern man in his own language; and he spoke to men, not to children, of their rights and dignity, of their innate sense of justice which they intuitively wish to see applied on an international scale, and of their human and spiritual freedom, without which nothing can be accomplished. The supreme Pastor deliberately rejected the dark pessimism so much in vogue. His words are not condemnatory; nor are they a list of abstract duties. Rather they are words to encourage modern men through this time which is difficult and decisive but which, like all times of great crisis, is also full of great hope and promise.

The appeal of the Pope is optimistic. The tone is similar to the open optimism of his inaugural address to the assembled fathers at the Second Vatican Council (October 11, 1962), in which he told them that this is a time of great opportunity and challenge for the Church, not one of pessimism. This optimism springs from a faith in free human nature, created by God and redeemed by Christ. Viewed in this perspective, the supreme dignity of man gave the Holy Father the serene confidence that he manifested throughout the encyclical.

John XXIII put an end, at least in theory, to the Catholic ghetto mentality which has been prevalent since the Reformation. The concept of the Church as an armed fortress fighting off the on-slaughts of the enemy is a thing of the past. The Pope told Catholics that they must become involved in the modern world, with all its particular problems. As Péguy once remarked, the reason so many Catholics do not have dirty hands is because they have no hands. The Pope appealed to Catholics to use their hands, and, echoing our Lord's words to his disciples, he urged Catholics to become the evangelical yeast in the modern world. The Pope had no fear of the modern world or of its achievements; he har-bored no nostalgia for a defunct ecclesiastical medievalism. On the contrary, he expressed the grandeur of modern man and pointed out how he can grow even greater and more firm. His words are an encouragement to further the ideals of modern man, and these words lean on the common dignity of man. In the words of the Jesuit martyr of World War II, Father Delp, "Man must be educated to resume his proper status of manhood, and religion must be taught intensively by truly religious teachers. The profession has fallen into disrepute and it will have to be re-established." What is needed, he added, is not simply good will and piety, but "truly religious men ready to co-operate in all efforts for the betterment of mankind and human order."[1]

This present commentary on the encyclical *Pacem in terris* of His Holiness Pope John XXIII is obviously incomplete. Larger commentaries and analyses are needed to explicate its manifold riches and teachings completely. We have thought, however, that a small commentary on the encyclical would be of use to those

[1] *The Prison Meditations of Father Delp* (New York: Herder & Herder, 1963), pp. 7, 10.

who do not have the time or resources for a more thorough study. As he reads, the reader ought not to look for more than what is here; this is only a rudimentary study of the highlights of the encyclical. The text of the encyclical which has been reprinted at the end of the book is that of the Paulist Press and the subtitles and paragraph numbers that head each of the sections in this book correspond to those of the papal document in this edition.

This commentary is the fruit of the social labor and thought of an individual author, and it is not proposed as the Holy Father's thought as such. It is an endeavor to understand his mind.

The author is particularly indebted to his brother, Frank Riga, in the preparation of this volume. Without his understanding assistance and criticism this book would never have been written.

East Aurora, New York   PETER RIGA

29

Part I
Order Between Men

FOR the first time in the history of papal encyclicals, a pope addressed an encyclical not simply to Catholic bishops and their subjects but "to all men of good will." John XXIII could address all men in this way because his observations and discussion are based on natural and moral law, discernible by every man who enjoys the use of reason. The notion of *natural law* has been a source of confusion for many non-Catholics; by natural law, the Holy Father meant that man has reason, and that he can use it to reflect upon experience. Pope John did not wish to give a course in the moral philosophy of natural law; he simply said that every man has reason, and by using it on the realities exposed in the encyclical, every man will derive more or less the same conclusions. He thus proposed his words to all men for consideration.

Order in the Universe and Order in Human Beings: ¶1–¶7

Man's destiny, in a true sense, is in his own hands under the providence of God. The main instrument which God has given man to accomplish his destiny is reason, which, correctly used, is an extension of God's providence, in St. Thomas' words.

The concept of the law of nature is by no means an invention of the Catholic Church, as is sometimes erroneously believed. Owing to this regrettable prejudice, certain schools of thought have rejected the essentially unanimous agreement of innumerable thinkers who affirm in the name of reason the validity of the supreme ideals of mankind. It would be superfluous to enumerate the many witnesses to the natural law, but a quick review of a few of their opinions will demonstrate that they are in agreement with the highest maxims of the Gospel, which proclaims as a principal thesis the universal brotherhood of man.

The idea of a necessary society of the human race and of its unity in reason appeared early in the philosophy of the Stoics. It was expressed splendidly in one of Cicero's celebrated passages:

> True law is right reason, harmonious with nature, diffused among all, constant, eternal; a law which calls to duty by its commands and restraints from evil by its prohibitions . . . . It is a sacred obligation not to attempt to legislate in contradiction to this law; nor may it be derogated from nor abrogated . . . .[1]

In a later age, Dante Alighieri said, "Totus humanum genus ordinatur ad unum," and Francisco Vitoria, "Totus orbis aliquo modo est una respublica." This list could be expanded by the addition of many other philosophers who, while following different methods in their proofs, support the postulate of the one great city of the world (Vico), or the *civitas gentium maxima* (Wolff), or the *Welterpublik* (Kant). It is unnecessary to recall other examples, including recent ones, that confirm this concept and that have never been validly refuted by those who reject it. Pope John XXIII was a continuation of this historic voice.

Man's only alternative to reason is to allow the prevalence of the arbitrary will of nations; between the two there are no intermediate solutions. If owing to antiphilosophic prejudice, universal truths dictated by reason are rejected and only the manifestations of the changing will of nations are revered, whatever these may be, it would be absurd to attempt the construction of a juridical organization of the human race, just as it would be a hopeless undertaking to build a house on moving sands.

[1] As quoted in Giorgio Del Vecchio's *Justice* (Edinburgh, 1956), pp. 5, 10, 18.

The Holy Father's discussion directly opposes many modern philosophical theories that view history as a deterministic convergence of irrational forces in nature. Deterministic views like these are not new. Recent studies of Greek, Hindu, Buddhist, and other concepts of history reveal this pessimistic determinism. The Greek idea of history, for example, was embedded in the theory of ever-recurring cycles. After innumerable years, the same events were bound to recur, for history had no end, no finality in itself. This notion reflected the eternal pessimism common to the Greek writers who predated Christ. Even Plato, or at least Plato as interpreted by his disciples, offered only the possibility of an intellectual passage from the world of time to the world of immutable ideas and essences. This possibility, however, did not come to grips with realities in time and space; it was merely a form of escape from this world.

If today's world possesses an authentic idea of history, then it owes that idea to Christianity. At one point in time, God made His entrance into the world of flesh and blood. From that time on, history has been invested with an end, a destiny, and having a destiny, it has sense and value. Christ has come and He will come again; the world has already entered eschatological time because it has received the token of the Spirit. The Kingdom of God is already present in embryo. Its full maturity is still awaited, but, as Cardinal Newman said, "If He tarry, He will surely come."[2] In a true theological sense, Christ has given a definitive meaning to history for the Christian. Compared to this, all other interpretations of history are either incomplete or dissatisfying for the deep-seated instincts of man. Father de Lubac sums up the argument clearly and concisely:

[2]See *A Catholic Catechism* (New York, 1957), p. 425.

Christianity alone affirms for man a transcendent destiny and for humanity as such a common destiny. All history in the world is a preparation for that destiny. From creation to the final consummation, through all the resistance of matter and of the free will of man, the same divine will will be fulfilled . . . . *Circuitus illi jam explosi sunt.* It is the triumphal cry of the Christian to whom God has been revealed as Creator and Saviour. The infernal circle of the Greeks has been destroyed. Historical facts are no longer just single phenomena, they have become events, acts, *gesta Dei.* There is a birth, an effective growth, a maturing of the universe. The world, having an end, has therefore sense, i.e., a direction and a signification. The whole human race is the child of God and all is sustained within the hands of God, and in the word by the Spirit, all is directed to the Father.[3]

Without this basic presupposition, it is difficult if not altogether impossible to give any sense to the history of mankind.

The Holy Father's view of history is not fatalistic or evasive. In his view, man is a free agent created in the image of God and has his destiny in his own hands. Man determines his own destiny under God; he is not a slave to instinct as are the animals, nor to the subconscious forces of his own being, nor to the irrational forces of society. To discover God's ways and laws, in which he can find true peace, man has been given the gift of reason, and only in the use of reason can he control his own destiny under God.

It is noteworthy that in an encyclical dedicated to peace so much emphasis is placed on the rights of man, more even than that placed on peace itself. The opening of the letter directly mentions peace, but in the encyclical as a whole the rights of man are more fully discussed than the idea of peace. This is not illogical, for peace would be an empty mockery without this basic

[3]*Catholicism* (London, 1955), p. 70.

recognition. Peace is the fruit of justice, animated by love of the objective order given by God. And justice demands above all the acknowledgment that the human person is endowed with liberty, that is, with a natural right which bestows perfect equality on all men. As Albert Camus said, "Without liberty it is possible to improve heavy industry, but not to increase justice or truth."[4] In accordance with the Holy Father's concept of justice, basic forms of social activity must have corresponding concrete legislative enactments, a prescription which elevates freedom to a universal application; but these enactments must always be in the best interest of various individual freedoms, such as freedom of thought, speech, work, and association. Part I of the encyclical considers the problem of justice generally and specifically.

In the world that science, technology, and education have created, the maintenance of existing inequalities represents a permanent threat to peace, especially in those areas where people feel, rightly or wrongly, that they are being deprived of their rights. Any advance in justice will advance peace. Yet the view that justice is merely a pragmatic means of maintaining peace is inadequate, and Pope John opposed such a view. In his vision, rights and the justice that corresponds to them are moral imperatives before they are political guarantees. If the moral outlook is lacking, rights are nothing more than capricious concessions by the state. Such a view, in reality, is the foundation of any totalitarian state. Pope John clearly states that "Peace on earth . . . can be firmly established only if the order laid down by God be dutifully observed" (¶ 1). Thus, in the thought of Pope John, justice—or, to use the term of many contemporary authors, social justice—is something that intrinsically pertains to all people

[4]Quoted in *Time*, vol. 75, no. 3 (Jan. 18, 1960), 28.

throughout the world. In this encyclical, it is evident that social justice means more than the fair production and distribution of economic goods. More comprehensive in his view, Pope John regarded man and his rights in a total fashion, and throughout *Pacem in terris,* justice includes the total way in which the whole cultural, moral, and spiritual heritage of humanity is created and made available to all men. It demands that each man and nation have access to the material and spiritual resources; this is necessary if human beings are to develop harmoniously. Furthermore, justice demands that those who are more advanced come to the aid of the less fortunate, as a man comes to the aid of his brother. Pope John stated this clearly in the earlier encyclical *Mater et Magistra:*

> The solidarity which binds all men and makes them members, in a sense, of the same family requires that nations enjoying an abundance of material goods should not remain indifferent to those nations whose citizens suffer from internal problems that result in poverty, hunger, and an inability to enjoy even the more elementary human rights. This obligation is all the more urgent since, given the growing interdependence among nations, it is impossible to preserve a lasting and beneficial peace while glaring socioeconomic inequalities persist among them.[5]

Justice is the result of love, for where there is no love, there can be no justice. Social justice is indivisible: as the individual treats one man, so he treats all men. This is so, says the Holy Father, because all men are members of one family, each depending on the other. At present, the world faces two formidable threats. On the one hand, a type of nationalism has arisen in some parts of the world that hinders progress; on the other, the division of the

---

[5]John XXIII's encyclical letter *Mater et Magistra,* in *Acta Apostolicae Sedis* (hereafter abbreviated *AAS*), LIII (1961), 409, ¶ 157 (Paulist trans.).

world into two opposing power blocs tends to check normal development, either by preventing needed changes or by modifying changes in accordance with the interests of the dominant powers. In either case, the result stifles justice. The passion for social justice is the only guarantee and safeguard of man's love of his fellow man; and without love or justice there can be no liberty or peace.

The functions of all states must conform with this concept of justice. The state has the duty of confirming and protecting rights, and this duty constitutes the first and unchallengeable condition of its existence, the justification of its activity, and the limit of its lawful authority over the individual. In the state, then, all forms of justice must be paramount. Further, all forms of justice have as their primary reason for existence the safeguarding and promotion of the individual person's rights. To illustrate this personalistic relation of justice and man, the Holy Father next delves into the nature of man.

Every Man Is a Person with Rights and Duties: ¶8–¶10

To understand the personalistic conception of man's rights, the nature of these rights must be examined closely. It is evident that the subject of these rights is the person himself precisely because, writes the Holy Father, he has intelligence and free will, and is thus capable of and responsible for the realization of his moral destiny. In man's personal being lies the source of his rights, and he is the bearer of these rights. These rights are *universal* because they pertain to every person on the face of the earth. Since these rights are not arbitrary, they pertain to what man is and to his fulfillment as a human person—they cannot be granted or denied by the whim of the state. They are *inviolable* and *inalienable* because each person has a destiny which no one else can take or fulfill for him; and if each man must fulfill his destiny, he must have the means, ensured by his fundamental rights, to do so. Therefore, it is only the individual person who is the subject of rights.

The law and the state exist only to promote, safeguard, and sometimes limit these rights for the greatest good of all. Even those who are not conscious of their rights, such as children, idiots, and the mentally ill, are subjects of rights, and these persons cannot be eliminated when they are no longer "useful" to the state or the economic community. Every person must be considered the subject of rights by the simple and undeniable fact that he is a person. From this fact, the Holy Father later concludes that every type of racism, extreme nationalism, or religious prejudice is a terrible evil. That a man is black or white, Christian or Jew, American or Japanese has no effect on the fact that he is a person and therefore must be treated always and everywhere with the dignity he deserves as a human being. Any other attitude on the part of a Catholic, at least, is doctrinal and spiritual error. As *Pacem in terris* states:

> . . . the conviction that all men are equal by reason of their natural dignity has been generally accepted. Hence racial discrimination can in no way be justified, at least doctrinally or in theory. And this is of fundamental importance and significance for the formation of human society . . . [¶ 44].

This recognition of human rights is an essential point in the building of any valid and lasting social or political world community. Without a recognition of these rights, there can be no mutual trust or confidence among the world's nations. In practice, if not in ideology, totalitarianism denies that the person is the subject of rights, claiming that only the state is the subject of rights. When the communists applauded the Pope's stand on peace and international disarmament, the Holy See had to remind them that the basis for this could only be a sincere and unconditional recognition of the human and civil rights of the person. If the totalitarian conception were true, the state would determine to whom it would give the "privilege" of exercising rights; that is, rights would simply be concessions given to the citizen by the state. The state alone would determine who lives and who dies, who is worthy to propagate life and who is to be sterilized, who learns and who remains ignorant. The consequences of such a foundation for any human community, national or international, would be appalling. Thus, the Holy Father says that this recognition of human rights is absolutely necessary if we are to speak of a really human community, *a fortiori* of the international community.

Any human society, if it is to be well ordered and productive, must lay down as a foundation this principle: that every human being is a person; his nature is endowed with intelligence and free will. By virtue of this, he has rights and duties of his own, flowing directly and simultaneously from his very nature, which are therefore universal, inviolable, and inalienable [¶ 9].

The Right to Life and a Worthy Manner of Living: ¶11

In his discussion of the material necessities of life, the Holy Father reveals an acute awareness of reality. Human rights are in constant danger not just from political power but equally from technical, economic, and other social institutions. In societies where the material standard of living is inadequate, the individual's faith in basic human rights is practically nonexistent. Yet another observation is in order here. Material poverty is not the only cause of individuals' losing their sense of the value and necessity of basic human rights; excessive comfort has exactly the same effect. Immured in luxury, a man may be all too ready to sacrifice his freedom to ensure his high material standard of living. This is a lesson often repeated in history.

Moreover, the Holy Father goes on to specify those rights which flow from the very nature of man and which cannot be denied by individuals or governments. In enumerating these particular rights, he moves from the more material to the more spiritual, which are equally essential.

> . . . every man has the right to life, to bodily integrity, and to the means which are necessary and suitable for the proper development of life; these are primarily food, clothing, shelter, rest, medical care, and finally the necessary social services. Therefore, a human being also has the right to security in cases of sickness, inability to work, widowhood, old age, unemployment, or in any other case in which he is deprived of the means of subsistence through no fault of his own [¶ 11].

The Holy Father developed most of the economic rights enumerated here in his encyclical *Mater et Magistra.*

Man is not simply a soul imprisoned within a body; he is an incarnate spirit, an incarnate interiority, and his body is an essential principle of his being. Only through his body does man have the possibility of doing good, of making his contribution to society, and of developing himself as a man, as God has willed him to develop. Therefore, life is a precious gift, and man has a right to it and must respect it. At times, he can even assert his

41

right to life against others who would unlawfully attempt to take it from him, that is, in self-defense.

The duration of his life is the framework for a man's activities toward his moral perfection. He must act according to the *objective meaning* of life, for example, by using the normal means demanded for health. Hence, he has the right to everything which is necessary for the preservation and advancement of life. The requirements of health include rest, leisure, and safety and hygienic conditions at work and elsewhere.

The interconnection of man's body and spirit is seen nowhere more clearly than in his need to work. The material rewards of his work supply his bodily wants, but there are other rewards which, though intangible and difficult to measure, are equally important; man needs to make a contribution to society, for example, and to fulfill his moral being by the development of his talents. These intangible rewards relate to spiritual values and are as necessary to man's growth as food.

From the right to a worthy standard of living, the encyclical proceeds easily to the rights to moral and cultural values.

Rights Pertaining to Moral and Cultural Values: ¶12–¶13

In his discussion of the rights pertaining to moral and cultural values, Pope John of necessity considers the adjuncts required for the fruition of truth and understanding: accurate information and an adequate education.

Underlying the affirmation of these conditions is a tacit assumption about the society in which they can exist. The type of society which has evolved since the late eighteenth century is that of political democracy. Today, even totalitarian states have this ideal written into their constitutions. The essence of democracy is a free citizenry under a limited government which safeguards the rights of all the members by law. Such a system of government is based on universal suffrage, which presupposes freedom of opinion and association, freedom of expression in speech or in print so that the truth or falsity of an idea can be tested in the public forum, freedom of communication, and other related freedoms. In order for a man to realize his duties toward the common good or toward his fellows, he must be free to communicate with others and to be informed truthfully about public events so that he can make an accurate and objective judgment of the events which are within his responsibility in a political democracy. Having formed his judgment, he must be free to propagate it and to join with others of similar persuasion. And under the auspices of universal suffrage, he may be able to make his opinion prevail. These specific rights are absolutely basic to any true democracy.

What is perhaps more fundamental is the right of citizens to an education in proportion to their talents. The reasons for this are numerous. A political democracy presupposes an educated citizenry which can understand issues, since it is the people who assume responsibility for the election of their representatives. But more important, a man has a right and an obligation to develop the talents which God has given him so that he may make a contribution to society with his unique genius. This can only be accomplished by education. Since each man has a right to an education to develop his talents, the only criterion must be his talents; if he cannot pay for his education, then the state has a responsibility to aid him.

43

Every right has its corresponding responsibility. Although it is true that responsibilities flow from human rights and not the reverse, the obligation to fructify talents remains. This is particularly true in the modern affluent society, where the ideal of giving oneself and one's talents to the public good is treated as a naive aspiration and the "what's-in-it-for-me" attitude is all too prevalent. The Holy Father states clearly that talents are God's gift to man, and that they are both individual and social in nature. A man must develop his talents, but he will find their perfection only when he uses them for the good of others in a social context. The primary concern, especially for the Christian, is how better to serve man with what God has given. Unfortunately, this type of social thinking is not overly common today, not even among Christians. The Christian has learned the individual dimension of piety and religious obligation; of his social dimension, however, he has little awareness.

The Right To Worship God According to an Upright Conscience: ¶14

For the first time in papal history, the principle of religious freedom is clearly embodied in the text of an encyclical. Pius XII mentioned this in his allocution to the Roman jurists, but the principle is stated clearly and authoritatively in *Pacem in terris*. Because man is free, he has an obligation to investigate and find the objective meaning of existence. Since he must direct his acts according to the judgment of conscience, he must form that judgment carefully, prudently, and in good faith. The fact that a person's conscience can be in error, despite his best endeavors, does not negate his duty of following it once its judgment is formed.

The norm of morality which must apply to human actions can only be derived from the judgment of conscience; and since this judgment can have only moral certainty, error is always possible. If man were not allowed to make any errors, action would be impossible, and action is necessary for him to reach his moral destiny. Man must follow his conscience, and this is a human right. This line of reasoning is sometimes objected to because error has no rights; but neither does truth. Strictly speaking, only a person has rights.

A person has the moral obligation to form his conscience according to objective truth, and he has performed that duty once he has formed his conscience, even though he only remains in the realm of moral certainty. Obviously, freedom of conscience does not consist in an arbitrary formation of conscience which excludes a consideration of objective truth. This is moral indifference and has been condemned by the Church. The Holy Father is not speaking of an arbitrarily formed conscience, but one which conforms as much as possible to objective truth. Other individuals and the state must respect both the private and public manifestations of this conscience.

What most moderns call the virtue of tolerance, which they feel is the fruit of contemporary understanding, is nothing more than a sentiment that religious truths are unimportant and therefore should not be quarreled over. This type of tolerance can never be accepted by any true Catholic or by anyone who respects truth. Tolerance is not a virtue; its existence merely stimulates the expression of virtue. For example, tolerance allows respect for the sincerely formed conscience of others. Tolerance is a passive or negative quality because its function depends upon the existence of an objective evil, that is, the existence of erroneous religious teachings. To be tolerant, a person must allow this error to exist, but if he is true to his own religious convictions, he must recognize that the error is error and not "as good as" his belief.

Tolerance permits the existence of erroneous religious teachings, and it forbids the inculcation of the faith by force. Though not very likely today, there is always the danger that certain forms of coercion could be applied. If any religious group, for example, succeeded in introducing inequities into the social, economic, or political order, a person might be tempted for purely pragmatic reasons to abandon his own religious convictions and embrace a faith in which he did not believe. To this argument some might object that men should have the courage of their convictions. Experience shows, however, that most men are not heroes and that it is unrealistic to expect heroic virtue from them. When enough external pressure is brought to bear, most men will not have the courage to resist. In countries where Catholics are a majority, for example, there is the possibility that they might create conditions which would jeopardize the freedom of conscience of non-Catholics. In his encyclical *Mystici Corporis Christi,* Pius XII warned against any such use of force:

Faith, without which no one can be pleasing to God, must be a completely free surrender of the understanding and the will. If therefore a case should ever arise in which someone were forced against his will into professing the Catholic faith—contrary to the constant teaching of this Apostolic See—We should be forced to disassociate Ourselves from such use of force, as Our duty.[6]

[6]Pius XII's encyclical letter *Mystici Corporis Christi,* in *AAS,* 38 (1943), pp. 391–392.

Freedom of conscience is the ultimate justification for allowing the existence of false religious teachings, and the need for this freedom is revealed in a proper understanding of the true nature of the Christian faith. A direct or indirect imposition of Catholicism by law is in direct conflict with the spirit of Christianity. In Christianity, the act of faith is a free act, on the part of God Who calls men and on the part of men who respond and give themselves to God. Sacred Scripture and Church tradition reveal that the act of faith brings the person of the believer and the Person of God into an intimate relationship. Faith, then, is a personal relationship between a human person and God; it is, in short, man's total gift of himself to God in a response of voluntary love. As St. Thomas states, "Belief depends on the will of the believer; but man's will needs to be prepared by God through grace, so that it may be raised to things which are above nature."[7]

Religious belief is the interior acceptance of some objective truth revealed to man by the authority of God. It is inconceivable that anyone could be forced to believe contrary to his own convictions, but the application of force could make a dissident's life so difficult that he would be tempted to disregard or act contrary to his conscience. This danger can be eradicated through a proper understanding of tolerance. In this regard, it is the state's strict duty to ensure effective freedom of conscience, of propagation of worship, and of teaching for all ideological groups, as long as they do not constitute a danger to the general welfare. Suarez pointed out the intrinsic evil in every direct constraint on non-believers, even if they were subjects of a Catholic state. Arguing from a concept of tolerance, he also insisted that civil authority must shun indirect constraints. Social and political life should be

[7]*Summa Theologica, II–II*, q. 6, a. 1, ad 3.

47

organized in a manner favorable to God's grace and faith as well as to human freedom. True faith can only flourish in an atmosphere free from religious restraint. Cardinal Feltin of Paris has summed up the problem in this way:

> Social pressure, spiritual emancipation—which will win? As a man, I cannot tell; as a bishop, I am bound to choose. And my choice is freedom. At a higher level than the disputes of the schools and political ideologies, freedom assumes a pastoral dimension. The reason is not exterior or secondary, as if the Church were claiming freedom only to accommodate itself to the taste of the day. Freedom lies at the heart of Christianity, which seen from without might look like a system, but thought and lived from within is a living bond between persons, a religion of the spirit. Faith is the encounter of a free gift and a free acceptance; a call on the part of God and a conscious and submissive response to God's voice. . . . Freedom for the sake of freedom, freedom for the sake of approaching nearer to God, such is the Christian order which is ours to promote.[8]

Consequently, any attempt by the state either to force or to disallow the act of faith is tantamount to its destruction. The obvious limits to this freedom are set by the common good; but freedom must always be dominant.

The problem of tolerance must now be considered from the standpoint of the objective content of faith. At one moment in time, God spoke to man through His only-begotten Son. The incarnation is a valid truth for all men for all time. It is the eternal truth of God Who has revealed Himself to men; it is an absolute truth, and God demands its acceptance. This truth has been entrusted to the Church, and objectively, all men who wish the fullness of divine truth must become members of the Church. Our Lord has commanded the Church to preach this truth to all men until the end of time: "Go into the whole world and preach

[8]*Christianity and Freedom* (London, 1955), pp. 159–162.

the gospel to every creature. He who believes . . . shall be saved"
(Mk 16:15). This is the mission of the holy Church until the
second coming of Christ, a mission accomplished by its preaching
and teaching authority. This is an absolute Catholic truth. Does
this truth, then, allow the Church to use all means, even force, to
favor her preaching and to spread the faith?

To answer this question, the end of the Church's preaching and
witness must be examined. The end is obviously that all men
might believe, that all men make the act of faith. As the First
Vatican Council described her, the Church is a sign elevated
among the nations so they might contemplate the spiritual beauty
and truth on which she is founded. Yet Christ did not use force
to win His followers; He appealed to their freedom. In the same
way, the means which the Church uses must be adapted to the
spiritual end which she seeks to accomplish. The act of faith is a
free and supernatural act, and the means employed to lead men
toward that act must respect its double character.

Hence the Church must appeal to man's freedom, enriched
and strengthened by God's grace. Force has absolutely nothing to
do with this appeal. The appeal must be that of Christ, Who
never used force and even rebuked Peter for attempting to use it.
Unambiguously, the Gospel of St. John teaches that God appeals
to man's freedom to choose Christ, Who manifested Himself in
signs of work and doctrine. The Church must be that "continued
sign" which appeals to men's minds and souls by the purity and
loftiness of her work and doctrine, for the Church is simply the
continuation of Christ's work and doctrine.

Catholic theologians have argued that the civil power may never
use force justly for the propagation of any religious faith. If the
Church is complete in its own sphere (as was stressed by Leo

XIII), then it becomes difficult indeed to understand how she or any religious body could justify an appeal to a secular authority to enforce her aim. The proper end of the civil authority is the public and temporal good of society, and the proper end of the Church is to lead all men to the faith. If this traditional teaching of Catholic canonists is true, it is impossible to use the civil power to promote the act of faith; no argument could be forwarded to justify an exception to this sacred distinction. At different times, some persons have proposed that the civil authority should serve the Church because, though the Church does not have direct power over the state, her end has superior dignity. This superior dignity is granted, but it proves nothing, because both ends remain distinct, one secular and the other spiritual. In the words of John Courtney Murray:

It may be that in a Catholic society heretical propaganda does spiritual harm. Granted: nevertheless, this is not the kind of harm that secular government, as an agent of public order, is bound by its office to ward off from its citizens. The protection of her members in the possession of their faith is the task of the Church; it is a spiritual, not a political task. And if the Church is too weak to perform this task successfully, she does not by that fact acquire a juridical right to invoke the coercive strength of secular government. If it be asserted that the temporal power is distinct from the spiritual power, sovereign in a limited order distinct from the spiritual power, it cannot be that the distinctions asserted should suddenly vanish to permit the temporal order to become attached to the Church as her "secular arm" to minister to needs that are not secular but spiritual.[9]

Hardly new, Father Murray's teaching can be traced to such ancient authors as Lactantius and Tertullian, both of whom argued that if a man is forced to the faith in any way, he is not

[9]"Government Repression of Heresy," *The Proceedings of the Third Annual Meeting of the Catholic Theological Society of America* (Chicago, 1948), pp. 67–68.

offering himself as God wills. Catholic tradition is full of such examples, and it is needless to cite more of them here.

Some general conclusions regarding the Catholic tradition of the act of faith and religious freedom are in order. The act of faith is a free response of the total man to God. Even when it is simply considered as knowledge, faith is an activity that engages the whole person, not merely his intellect. As the work of Cardinal Newman demonstrates, this total effort is necessary because the knowledge of faith touches man's interiority, his very being, since it permits him to know of the existence of an entirely new end to human life. In the Christian tradition, then, man's freedom and God's gratuitous call are foremost. One famous theologian concludes:

> . . . the reception of the word of God ought not just to put into action my speculative faculty but also my whole personality and liberty; this is true because it is a question—in the act of faith—of being a listener to *someone* and not to something or a thought; we must speak of the "thou" and not of the "it"; yet, we formally listen to a person only in the act where one consents freely to such an act, i.e., to give or refuse one's whole being.[10]

Martin Buber, the Jewish theologian, has also focused attention on this "I-Thou" relationship between the believer and God.

In its early tradition as well as in the Scholastic period, the Church always called faith the *substantia rerum sperandarum*. This same point was made by the Council of Trent (1545–1563) when it affirmed that the first object of the adult convert's faith was his justification through God's gratuitous grace. St. Thomas makes the same point. Thus, in the Pauline sense of the word, faith is the personal and firm attachment of the Christian to the

[10]L. Malcolm, "Théologie Dialectique" in *Revue de Science Religieuse,* 28 (1938), p. 387.

person of Christ, the Lord and Master. And throughout the Christian tradition, the act of faith has been "the beginning of eternal life in us."[11]

All of the above leads to an extremely simple conclusion. Given this personal and intimate faith, this dialogue between the human person who responds and the Person of God Who calls him to the new life, any kind of force—direct or indirect—is nothing short of sacrilege. Human coercion is incapable of eliciting the act of faith, and any attempt to do so is a flagrant violation of the supernatural character of faith, the dignity of the human person, and the free initiative of God Himself.

But the true Catholic can never accept the idea that liberty of conscience means the freedom to believe or disbelieve anything he chooses. All men are bound by the objective truth immutably revealed through Christ. In this sense, doctrinal error has no objective validity, and it therefore cannot claim adherence from anyone. Some argue that since error has no rights it should not be tolerated. But this is to put an intricate question in a poor perspective. Of course error has no rights, but persons do, even if they are in error. Although men are bound in the objective order to accept God's revelation as proposed by the Church, the formal morality of any action is measured by the dictates of conscience at the moment the act is performed.

Since it is now inopportune to investigate the notion of erroneous conscience, let it suffice to say that when a conscience is honestly formed, whether it corresponds to objective truth or not, it must be followed under penalty of sin. This is the conclusion reached by the great Scholastics of the thirteenth century as well as by traditional Catholic theology. In the words of St. Thomas,

[11]*Summa Theologica,* II–II, q. 1, a. 7.

"We must therefore hold, without qualification, that whether the reason be correct or mistaken, the will which is at variance with it is always evil."[12] This conclusion, however, does not reduce the importance of the objective norm. Catholic theologians have always emphasized man's grave moral obligation to form his conscience according to God's objective revelation.

Yet because of circumstances beyond his control, an individual may be ignorant of the true objective norm, and in an honest and sincere way he may have formed his conscience according to what is objectively incorrect. In such a case, his conscience must direct his actions, since he has no other way of knowing God's will. Pius XI states it this way: "We are both proud and happy to fight for the liberty of consciences, not indeed (as someone, perhaps inadvertently, has quoted Us as saying) for the liberty of conscience which is an ambiguous expression that is all too often wrongly used to mean complete independence of conscience, which is absurd when applied to a soul created and redeemed by God."[13]

The Right To Choose Freely One's State of Life: ¶15–¶17

The right to choose a vocation in life flows from the fact that a man is irreplaceable. No one can take his place; no one can act in his stead. It is true that others can and should aid him to attain his full stature through education, but this is a human influence which is exterior. In the final analysis, only through his own acts and according to the originality and talents which God has given him can a man perfect himself. He has an obligation, and there-

[12]As quoted in E. D'Arcy, *Conscience and Its Right to Freedom* (New York, 1961), p. 108.
[13]"Non Abbiamo bisogno," in *AAS,* 23 (1931), 301–302.

fore a right, to develop these by his own initiative. From his right of personal initiative, he takes his own destiny into his hands. He therefore has the right to choose the vocation which best suits his originality and talents. Teachers, priests, and parents may guide youth, suggesting various ways for the development of talents, but they can never use direct or indirect means to force a child to follow any vocation.

As many popes have emphasized, marriage and the family are at the center of any healthy society. Therefore, the state has a grave obligation to protect and promote family life. In Christianity, however, a higher dimension of being is known through revelation: some are called to forgo marriage, the normal way of attaining human and divine perfection, and give themselves in an extraordinary way in the priesthood or the religious life.

In the Christian conception of existence, every vocation remains essentially a right, a responsibility, and a grace. Knowing the complex nature of the right to choose one's state in life, Pope John's discussion continues with an examination of economic rights, the logical concomitants to the right of selecting a vocation.

Rights Pertaining to Economic Life: ¶18–¶22

A man has the right of free initiative because of his originality and irreplaceability. From this follows man's right and obligation to work so that he may make his contribution to society. *Work* is to be understood in its broadest sense: it is not just financially productive activities but every activity which promotes all aspects of a culture.

In discussing work, authors distinguish between objective and subjective culture. Objective culture is the objective elements which are realized by human labor and which transform the world, that is, art, architecture, painting, writing, technology in all its forms, and so on. Subjective culture is the culture of the person himself, the fact that he perfects himself scientifically, intellectually, culturally, morally, and in every way possible to a human being. Obviously, there is a reciprocity between objective and subjective culture: the very reason objective culture exists is to promote the development of a person's subjective culture, so that he can realize his proper originality. Through this enrichment of each unique person, objective culture is in turn made richer.

Work is a noble thing, a furthering of God's creating act, and it is the means of bringing about objective values which men need for the development of subjective culture. The realization of culture is therefore a social task in which everyone must make his contribution according to his capacities. This is the basis of the duty of work and therefore of man's right to work. Because man's work is his contribution, by it he should be able to earn what is necessary for him to maintain his and his family's dignity. This demand was brought out clearly in *Mater et Magistra*.

Another important point brought out in *Pacem in terris,* as it was in *Mater et Magistra,* is that private property is a right. This right, however, is subordinate to the more fundamental right of all men to use the world's goods. Because men are incarnate spirits and must use material goods, all things have been created for their well-being. The goods of this world correspond to man's needs, and to live as a human being and to perfect his person he must make use of them. And if he *must,* he has a right to do so. This right of usage is the fundamental and primary right with regard to material goods. The right to property is secondary and derived, and it exists so that an order might be established in which the right of usage is assured. The right of property is a means to an end, and it is therefore subordinate to the right of usage. Because every means is necessarily relative, the doctrine of the absolute right of property is a grave social aberration. Private property must promote the right of usage. Thus, large land holdings in the hands of a few Latin Americans is a grave disorder because the right of usage is denied to the many. Property is a responsibility; it must be used to promote the general welfare.

From this discussion of the right to private property and the right of usage, it becomes obvious that rights are interconnected and that a right must always function within its proper sphere. The social nature of rights indicates something about society and man's behavior in it. The encyclical next enumerates some of the rights necessary for a proper society and man's proper behavior in it.

The Right of Meeting and Association; and the Right to Emigrate and Immigrate: ¶23–¶25

What seems at first sight to be evident—that all men are social by nature—results in some startling consequences when it is viewed as a right. If this is a right, then men are morally obliged to enter the political and cultural community and to cooperate for the common good. To understand man's social nature, it may be helpful to examine the Thomistic conception of society and of man's nature.

Man, says St. Thomas, is limited by his very nature; he is limited by time and by his capabilities. Because the individual cannot do everything at once, he must omit; he must do one thing and leave the rest for other men. A man's talents are also limited—he might have artistic but not technical abilities. It is impossible for one man to realize all of the values of his culture. Therefore, men need to cooperate, for no one man, no nation, no continent is sufficient to itself, especially in this age of international dependency.

In building a sane society, then, two things must be kept firmly in mind. First, man is an open being, open to himself, to others, and to God. He is an incarnate spirit, a person with infinite dignity. This is a fundamental value common to all men, and it must be respected if any political order is to lead to true peace. Through love, a man recognizes this fundamental equality among all men, and because of this equality, men can cooperate in the common good. Second, because of man's diversity and originality, the human community can progress and become richer. Each man realizes his possibilities in his own way because no two men are exactly the same. Through their diverse talents, men can realize many different aspects of human culture for the common enrichment of all the members of the community.

Human culture is thus a social reality wherein each man gives and receives in reciprocal enrichment. Each man is diverse, and this means a gain for all. In all social life, there is thus a kind of paradox. Human culture and society are possible only insofar as men are equal but also insofar as they are different. Equality is an indispensable condition of human society. Without diversity, however, there could be no human culture, because no one man can perform all of the tasks necessary to society. In this sense, diversity unites us. Thus, any true human community, national or international, has three component parts: many people live together; in their equality, limitations, and diversity, they cooperate in realizing human culture; and this culture is directed toward the individual perfection and development of each member.

To encourage the development of human diversity, the formation of many groups in a particular society is needed. From this need comes the right of man to form smaller associations in which to develop his talents. The corresponding right to move from one country to another when he cannot advance his economic and cultural development in a particular milieu or country is also derived from the need to encourage human diversity. Because he belongs to the human race, an individual's right and duty to immigrate flows from this relation to the human race and the enrichment of the world community.

One of the obvious realities in the organization of human equality and diversity is the political order, and since all men live in one political order or another, certain rights and obligations arise from this condition.

Rights in the Political Order: ¶26–¶27

Once again, the Holy Father emphasizes the priority of the rights of the human person over any arbitrary claim made by the state or by other individuals. This is the bedrock for the structure of any political community; arbitrary arrest, search, and wiretapping are all infringements on this priority. As the English tradition of law correctly insists, a man is innocent until proven guilty. In any society where the primacy of the human person prevails, the citizen has rights and civil liberties, and the burden of proof for the curtailment of these rights lies squarely on the authority which wishes to curtail them. The Fourteenth Amendment of the United States Constitution makes this point unambiguously:

No state shall make or enforce any law which shall abridge the privileges or immunities of citizens . . . nor shall any state deprive any person of life, liberty, or property, without due process of law; nor deny to any person within its jurisdiction the equal protection of the laws.

The Holy Father praises this modern trend toward limited government which incorporates human rights into laws, constitutions, and bills of rights.

In this regard, the United States is in a privileged position. The primacy of the human person in our laws and Constitution is a great contribution to the world. The Declaration of Independence, the Constitution which limits government, and the Bill of Rights are ideals for the international political community. It is particularly encouraging to see that the fundamental principles of these American documents conform exactly to those of the United Nations Charter, of UNESCO, and of the Universal Declaration of Human Rights. The Holy Father himself singles out this last document for special praise.

An act of the highest importance performed by the United Nations Organization was the Universal Declaration of Human Rights, approved in the General Assembly of December 10, 1948. In the preamble of that Declaration, the recognition of and respect for those rights and respective liberties is proclaimed as an ideal to be pursued by all peoples and all countries [¶ 143].

Time and again the Holy Father restates the basis of any human society, whether it be familial, national, or international: the rights of the human person, which, when guaranteed and promoted by positive laws and constitutions, are called civil rights. This point is the very heart and soul of the Holy Father's thought.

The reason for any human community or any government is the promotion and guarantee of the civil liberties of the human person. In the Declaration of Independence, these rights are called *inalienable* because they come from God and are therefore beyond the reach and tampering of men and government. To secure and promote these rights, governments are instituted among men, and government is legitimate only to the extent that it guarantees civil rights. In other words, a legitimate government provides the conditions in which men can exercise their natural rights. To disregard this philosophical and ethical structure is to eviscerate the thought of the Holy Father as well as to contradict the whole Western tradition of democratic, constitutional law.

Throughout the Holy Father's consideration of human rights, he maintains that persons have not only rights but also the corresponding obligations that arise out of these rights. The next part of his discussion specifies the dual nature of rights in their personal and interpersonal implications.

Rights and Duties Necessarily Linked in the One Person; Reciprocity of Rights and Duties Between Persons; Mutual Collaboration; and an Attitude of Responsibility: ¶28–¶34

Man is a social being because of his equality ("which draws its indestructible moral force from the natural law"[14]) and his diversity, but these gifts are given to him and to others to be enjoyed in mutual respect. In the spiritual life, man finds himself by giving of himself, and this is also true in the social life. Man's equality ensures his dignity; his diversity ensures his individual

[14]*Pacem in terris,* ¶ 157.

development and his contribution to society. Therefore, talents and abilities are a responsibility for each man. For example, a man has the right of education to develop himself as a human person, and because he has received from the learning of others, he also has the obligation to give of his developed talents for the enrichment of others. By this fact, a false libertarianism based on egoism has no place in the social field. Mutual sharing is the ideal of Catholic social justice.

From the dual nature of rights, the Holy Father derives other concomitants, especially the need for mutual cooperation in the promotion and protection of rights. He encourages all men to defend the rights of all in the community. *Civil liberties* has become a rather dirty phrase in certain American (and Catholic) circles. The Pope tells men that it is not sufficient to give lip service to a bill of rights, a constitution, or a universal declaration of human rights; each person must actively promote these human rights, not just for himself (as has too often been the case) but impartially for all men. Without this supreme test of action, the love of man becomes empty verbiage and hypocrisy, and the society will be in grave danger from a sinister type of subversion that gnaws away at its foundation: the slow disintegration of human rights. And surely no man can permit the denial of human rights by force; even silence in such circumstances gives the lie to our support of human rights.

Any human society perpetrates a terrible crime when it represses or makes difficult the exercise and full development of its citizens' equality and diversity. The ideal of civil law and government is to facilitate the practice of human rights, not to impede them. Laws aimed at such an obstruction are against the moral law and are therefore immoral; they are no law. But action and law that are based on truth and justice, explains the Holy Father, "continually give life."

Social Life in Truth, Justice, Charity, and Freedom: ¶35–¶36

Throughout this first and fundamental part of the encyclical, two characteristics are dominant. First, the Holy Father's philosophical and moral arguments can be substantiated by reason alone. As will be shown later, this fact allows great latitude to the Catholic for active cooperation with other Christian and non-Christian groups. Second—and this continues throughout the encyclical—the Holy Father's thought is personalistic, and the rights and the dignity of the individual human person are its essential core. This second characteristic will stand a little more explanation.

In the biblical tradition, man is the image of God insofar as he is an interiority and an intentionality; that is, he knows himself to be a moral being capable of controlling his destiny and of giving his existence a meaning. He seeks his moral perfection freely and consciously, and by that fact he has the obligation to become more and more like God. Even an atheist, in a sense, can understand his duty and responsibility to achieve moral perfection. For the atheist, the end of the perfection will be different from that for a Christian, but even he can reason that man is different from the rest of creation and that he attains his dignity and end freely and consciously. Yet for the atheist all would be relative, at least in the sense that the personalistic view of man cannot be absolute and must end with death. Without God, the goal or end of man is relative. But both the atheist and the Christian have the moral obligation to respect the infinite dignity of man. The Christian, however, goes further: his aspiration is to become more and more like God because it is God's will. In the supernatural order, the natural is not destroyed but rather transformed; the Christian is given a new motive for his participation in the world. God's gratuitous call to a superior life in grace animates his human activities by the more powerful motive of divine love.

The Moral Order Has Its Objective Basis in God: ¶37-¶38

The Holy Father was certainly one of the most forward-looking men of our time. Without nostalgia for a past culture or a past historical situation of the Church, he embraced fully and without reserve everything good and everything conducive to good in modern man. Many who have thought that the Church would always be doomed "to come too late" should be surprised at the depths of Pope John's vision of society. While not substituting earth for heaven in any terrestrial messianism (as is the case with much of Marxism), he saw the earthly city with a biblical vision, reflecting, in an imperfect but real way, the celestial city of God. This vision is what theologians during the past fifty years have called a theology of terrestrial realities.

Through sanctifying grace, the Christian has a foretaste and a beginning of eternal life here on earth, but this interior renovation must affect the earthly city in an attempt to bring about a reflection of that love, justice, truth, and freedom which will be fully realized in the heavenly city alone. A love which is based on the eternal truth of man's divine image and his God-given dignity produces a justice whose end is the peace and freedom of the sons of God.

In *Pacem in terris,* the Holy Father thus pictures the earthly city as a place where man's responsibility is to continue God's creation; this responsibility was originally given in Genesis, when God created man "to dominate the earth, the birds and the sea." And this duty is, as he says, "a spiritual reality." In the Pauline sense, the spiritual is not the mental or the intellectual opposed to the material, but it is the totality of man, both body and soul, living under and by the moral law that God has inscribed in his very nature. This duty to continue God's creation is spiritual, then, only in the biblical sense, since it is directed by the Holy Spirit of God. The only way that this duty can be accomplished is for all men of good will to recognize the will of God; and this is nothing more than a recognition of His moral law, which proclaims that man is created in His image. If this order is respected, then freedom and peace can ensue.

Characteristics of the Present Day: ¶39–¶45

The three characteristics of the present day that the Holy Father mentions have this in common: they are held together by the recognition of the human person's sacred rights. According to a sane moral philosophy, man is both an interiority and an intentionality. He alone is endowed with intelligence and free will, and without man there could be no significance or meaning in the world. But this meaning must be the one that God intended. Man must endeavor to discover what the Holy Father calls the *moral* meaning of things. Man does not create this; he simply discovers it by reason.

What does man discover when he applies his reason to reality? As already shown, men are equal and they are different or original. Because they participate in the same human nature, all men are equal. And since each man realizes himself and his existence in his own way, he is an originality. In any simple discussion among men, a diversity of personality is immediately evident. As a distinct individual, a man has a certain temperament, a certain sex, and certain tendencies and capacities; what he makes of these will determine his personality. Simply, then, man is a *person;* he must never be treated as an *object.* Karl Marx was right when he wrote in *Das Kapital* that the workers of his time were being used as objects of gain by the capitalists. Man is not an object, and he must never become the means by which others enrich themselves. The Holy Father concludes that the modern age is characterized by a strong emphasis on man's personality. He is not an object to be used, but a person.

From a positive point of view, other persons are to be treated as equals and as original. The Holy Father points out that the outstanding example of this is woman. Equal to man, she participates fully in the rights and responsibilities that are hers. In the past, however, she was treated as an inferior or a minor in a male society, even in Christian countries and by Christian thinkers. The modern age can no longer tolerate this inequality. Woman has an originality by the very fact of her sexual existence as a woman, and from this vantage point the originality of half of the world has barely begun to emerge. But it must emerge because it is woman's right.

The problem of woman's function in society has received much consideration from Catholic thinkers in the past few years, largely because of the many positions and responsibilities that women have acquired in recent times. The popes have considered this question, and their comments have been collected by the monks of Solesmes in a book entitled *Woman in the Modern World*. In this book, the comments of Pius XII take up 375 pages, while those of Leo XIII, Benedict XV, and Pius XI together only take up 41 pages. From this it is obvious that an awareness of the problem is relatively recent.

The problem of woman was recently examined by the French Existentialist, Simone de Beauvoir, in her book *The Second Sex*. After giving credit to Christianity for all that it has done for woman, she delivers a diatribe against the "slaveries" to which men, and especially Christian men, have subjected women. Women are passive, tied down domestically and bodily; they are restricted in their social and civic life.

This does not mean that many of her criticisms are not valid.

Her denunciation of the distorted conception of women in certain Christian circles is justifiable. The history of woman in human institutions demonstrates one clear fact: she has been treated as an inferior to man. The novelty of Christianity was that it declared the absolute spiritual equality of man and woman before God. This equality is evident in any study of the Gospels and Epistles. But an understanding and promotion of the social extensions of this aspect of Christian doctrine came slowly.

The main role of woman will always be motherhood, be it physical or spiritual. Common sense dictates that good men seldom come from unhealthy families. To a great degree, a man is what his mother has made him, and it is quite true that "the hand that rocks the cradle rules the world." In Christianity, however, maternity is not restricted to a physical relationship. Thousands of virgins are consecrated to the love of Christ in and through their femininity as teachers, nurses, missionaries, and social workers, and without their services the Church of the modern world would be less rich.

But the social structure of society has changed. In his discourse of October 21, 1945, Pius XII stated that while the main concern of women will always be the home, it is not for all women, nor must it be their only concern. Although woman is in no way inferior to man, he explained, she is complementary to man in her psychological, physiological, and spiritual qualities, and this must be respected if she is to engage profitably in the activities open to her in the modern world. All efforts to create a vulgar "equality" or to reduce her to performing the same tasks in the same way as men must be avoided, or her apostolate will be nullified. Socially awakened, women know the beneficial role they can play in the modern world. In fact, the Christian woman must accept this role with resolution; her mission has become an indispensable factor of civilization and progress.

Woman must accomplish this, however, in conformity with the specific talents that God has given her. Woman is and always will be essentially maternal. She must develop herself as a mother, caring for persons, not things, striving to bring about their happiness, and always seeking their good.

The tasks open to woman's delicate qualities are without number. The functions of the teacher and the nurse have always been a suitable choice for women because of their solicitude for children and the weak. Women as psychologists are a remarkable group because of their acute understanding of childhood disturbances. As social workers, they are without peers. Politics is certainly a vocation in which more women should participate. Women's sense of social justice, their personal responsibility, and their moral demands on society form a valuable counterbalance to the comparative coldness of "rational" men. Poetry and literature await the genius of women to bring out the beauty and order of the human condition.

All these are proper functions, and the list is by no means complete. One thing, however, is certain: today's Christian woman cannot confine herself exclusively to the home; her possibilities are unlimited because she shares responsibility with man for the progress and good of humanity. But humanity will profit from woman's participation only if she recognizes what she is and what she has been given. She is essentially a mother, and she exists for beneficial service to others.

A similar type of problem besets the newly formed nations. Since the end of World War II, more than a billion and a half people have received national independence. This is a great good. Too long in the past were they, like the workers of the nineteenth century, treated as objects for exploitation by the so-called Christian nations of Europe. The tale of colonization is too long and too repulsive to be related here; it is sufficient to say that these new nations have the right to develop themselves to the greatest possible degree, for each has a proper originality and genius through which it can contribute to the human family. Simply and directly, the Holy Father tells the newly emerging nations that the time of colonization is forever gone, and that they must now set themselves to the difficult task of constructing their political, economic, social, and cultural life. These millions of people understand and applaud this type of forthright and clear language.

Yet the Holy Father states that the main virtue which will cause men to recognize each other's originality is love. But what is love? Love is that virtue by which man values and esteems others as persons, as subjects and not objects. Love causes men to respect one another as equals and as original beings. As Corneille, the great French playwright, said: "Love creates equalities, it does not seek them." Love is not feelings, for feelings belong to the realm of tendencies which are not free. Love is an action of the intellect and the will whereby men esteem each other as equals. But esteem for the person is only a disposition, the interior aspect of love; more is demanded to have a true definition of love. Love is an *efficacious* act of the will. It does not simply esteem the qualities of another, but it tries to do something about it. Thus, love is a will to promotion.

Love is an appeal to another's liberty in order to help him become what he is capable of becoming. In this respect, the modern approach to education is not entirely false. The fundamental idea of helping the child to develop his proper initiative and capabilities is very good. In true love the teacher or parent makes an appeal to the capabilities of the child. In the same way and in every other domain, man cannot be forced; he must be freely led to see the good and to accomplish it. Any other system of ruling and governing is tyranny and a denial of the freedom of the sons of God. The Holy Father deals with this point when he discusses authority in Part II of the encyclical.

Love must result in respect for the originality of the person or nation. Parents must not force their children in any particular direction; the state must not force its citizens by creating difficulties for the exercise of various rights. Diversity in education, politics, ideas, and all other areas of life must be respected as a source of wealth and strength in any sane social order. When the state indirectly taxes a private system of education out of existence, for example, its action is a source of impoverishment for society and an injustice to all of the citizens.

Finally, love demands at least some type of reciprocity. All love perfects, and in this sense there is always reciprocity, even if there is no real personal exchange. Disinterested love is man's greatest opening to reality, and so the more disinterested man's love is, the more perfect he becomes. A man realizes his humanity as he gives himself to others in a disinterested way. This is true even when the other person cannot return love, as in an act of charity done in secret or in nursing an unconscious patient. This reciprocity, however, will attain its greatest degree when there is a mutual recognition, esteem, and will of promotion between two people.

Such a conception, according to the Pope, should be the soul of social life, and in it justice takes on its true meaning, whether it be with regard to persons, nations, or the whole human family. Justice is present in the relations between two people (or societies) by means of an external reality (the Scholastics called this *medium rei*). When a man buys a loaf of bread, his relationship with the baker is by means of a thing, the bread. The object of justice is this *medium rei* which is essential for the existence of love. Justice demands those external and objective elements necessary for love. Without this essential minimum, the other is treated as an object and not as a person. If the bread is offered at an exaggerated price, the baker makes this person an object of his personal greed.

In all events, man must avoid treating others as objects. Modern philosophers call this the recognition of man by man, and this recognition is the *object* of justice: it is the extension of a man's love for his fellow man made concrete and incarnate. This is what the Holy Father means when he says that charity in truth produces the fruit of justice and brings forth a true order of peace and freedom for all men of any color, creed, and sex.

Concluding his statement on the equality of all men, the Holy Father delivers some strong comments on racial discrimination.

On the contrary, the conviction that all men are equal by reason of their natural dignity has been generally accepted. Hence racial discrimination can in no way be justified, at least doctrinally or in theory. And this is of fundamental importance and significance for the formation of human society according to those principles which We have outlined above. For if a man becomes conscious of his rights, he must become equally aware of his duties. Thus, he who possesses certain rights has likewise the duty to claim those rights as marks of his dignity, while all others have the obligation to acknowledge those rights and respect them [¶ 44].

The consequences of the Holy Father's teaching are evident. Every type of racial bias and discrimination is intrinsically evil because it opposes the moral law. The Holy Father's words should be an unambiguous answer to the Catholics in New Orleans who once made an appeal to the Pope to justify their intolerance. They should also be clear to all men in South Africa, in Angola, in Oxford, Mississippi, and everywhere, for the teaching is based on the moral law, common to all men for all times and places. Since men are equal, each has rights and obligations which all other men must recognize. In other words, the argument is brought back to the rock-bottom basis of any worthy human society: the inalienable, universal, and inviolable rights of the human person. Racial discrimination in thought, teaching, and practice is intrinsically evil. In Pope John's words, our willingness to promote the rights of all men, weak or strong, rich or poor, black or white, is the supreme test of our commitment to Christ and to man. It will be the test of our preaching or of our hypocrisy: there is no middle road.

This paragraph of the encyclical will probably receive the greatest attention from American Catholics. The struggle against racial discrimination is taking a definite turn in our day and will continue with added intensity in the next few years. For the first time in American history, the Negro is ascending to the rank of first-class citizenship. In a real sense, this has been accomplished by the Negro himself. Outside of such eminent figures as Dorothy Day, Father John Lafarge, Archbishop Rummel, Cardinal Ritter, and a few others, Catholics in this fight have been conspicuous by their absence. Without belaboring the obvious, since the situation is much too serious for breast-beating, one example will demonstrate the point: at the first National Conference on Religion and Race held in Chicago in 1963, there was an open admission of the Christian failure in this regard. But because they have begun to realize this failure, Christians have begun to take positive steps to remedy the situation. There now exists a mild optimism, and all is not lost. In *Discrimination and the Christian Conscience,* the American bishops posed the challenge magnificently:

We hope and earnestly pray that responsible and sober-minded Americans of all religious faiths, in all areas of our land, will seize the mantle of leadership from the agitator and the racist. It is vital that we act now and act decisively. All must act quietly, courageously, and prayerfully before it is too late.[15]

The words are serious, but the challenge is too great to be ignored.

[15]Statement of the American Hierarchy issued in November, 1958. Reprinted from NCWC edition sheet (Washington, D.C., 1958).

The American weakness does not lie so much in having allowed the development of a missile gap but in having allowed the development of the moral gap that now exists between what is preached and what is practiced in regard to our fellow man. This is not pious verbiage. In an exhaustive and impartial sociological study called *The Religious Factor,* Gerhard Lenski examines the religious attitudes of a large cross-section of people living in metropolitan Detroit. He found that over fifty percent of the Christians queried would refuse to accept Negroes into their neighborhoods. Many, no doubt, were deceived by the specious argument about devaluation of property, but the terrible indictment remains.

The solution is not easy for the white American to accept because it involves a complete change in attitude toward Negro citizens. Most arguments against Negro equality are pure emotionalism, and herein lies the problem. Emotionalism cannot be reasoned with; it can only be checked by law and force. This is not enough. The white American needs a *metanoia* in the profound biblical sense of the term. He needs a change of heart, a re-examination of his attitudes in the light of the Holy Father's words and in those of the American bishops. The problem is basically moral, not legal or economic.

In this encyclical, the Holy Father has already pointed out that all of the rights of man come from the moral order; therefore, all men have the moral obligation not only to recognize them but also to be active in their promotion for all men in society. In the United States, this means concretely that Christians must actively participate to ensure that the Negro has equal employment rights, equal and adequate housing, equal educational opportunities, and equal protection for his human and civil rights before the law.

Though it has been said often, it bears another repetition: the time for Christians to act is now, before it is too late.

The concluding paragraph of this section of the encyclical concentrates the central idea of Part I in a brief statement.

When the relations of human society are expressed in terms of rights and duties, men become conscious of spiritual values, understand the meaning and significance of truth, justice, charity, and freedom, and become deeply aware that they belong to this world of values. Moreover, when moved by such concerns, they are brought to a better knowledge of the true God Who is personal and transcendent. Thus, they make the ties that bind them to God the solid foundations and supreme criterion of their lives, both of that life which they live interiorly in the depths of their own souls and of that in which they are united to other men in society [¶ 45].

Such a forceful elucidation of the infinite worth of the human person and of his sacred rights cannot be found in any previous papal document. The whole encyclical letter is constructed on the basis of accepting the rights of man in the moral order. Part I of the encyclical is a foundation for the other four parts. The structure of the letter rises on this first section. Its importance cannot be exaggerated.

Part II

Relations Between Individuals and the Public Authorities Within a Single State

AFTER discussing the foundation of the moral order, which is the recognition both in theory and fact of the rights of men, the Holy Father proceeds to analyze the relationship which should exist between the individual and the state. In Part II, the foundation of the moral order becomes the premise from which the Holy Father builds his argument; and in this argument, the essential and only function of any state is simply to safeguard, protect, and promote the rights of man for the common good.

Part II of the encyclical, then, is an examination of the meaning of state authority, which comes from God for the purpose of promoting and protecting human and civil rights. John XXIII quotes Pius XII with approval: "That same absolute order of beings and their ends . . . presents man as an autonomous person, that is, as the subject of inviolable duties and rights, and as at once the basis of society and the purpose for which it exists . . . ."[1] The purpose of the political community is to aid the individual in the exercise of his originality, not to supplant or replace him. All social legislation must allow the individual citizen a greater exercise of his freedom—economic, social, cultural, intellectual, and religious.

An essential function of the state is to ensure an equitable use of all resources so that an atmosphere of freedom can prevail. In this atmosphere, the citizen is liberated from inhuman and brutalizing work and from oppressive social forces which hinder the exercise of conscience and religion. He is liberated from the slavery of ignorance by the unimpeded flow of written and

[1]Pius XII's radio broadcast on Christmas Eve, 1944, *AAS*, XXXVII (1945), 15: quoted in *Pacem in terris* ¶ 47.

spoken information, the purpose of which is to ensure that all "persons be enabled, on the basis of merit, to go on to higher studies, so that, as far as possible, they may occupy posts and take on responsibilities in human society in accordance with their natural gifts and the skills they have acquired" (¶ 13).

With these tools of knowledge, all are to participate in public life, so that they can consciously and freely assume the responsibility of their social and political destinies. In the words of Pope John, "The dignity of the human person involves the right to take an active part in public affairs and to contribute one's part to the common good of the citizens" (¶ 26). The state authority must coordinate all these rights with their corresponding obligations so that each person will be able to make his contribution to the common good. This is the essence of any true authority in a human community:

> Inasmuch as individual men and intermediate groups are obliged to make their specific contributions to the common welfare, it especially follows that they should bring their own interests into harmony with the needs of the community. They should direct their goods and services toward goals which the civil authorities prescribe, in accord with the norms of justice ... [¶ 53].

Part II of the encyclical is a consideration of the ways and means that the public authority must use to promote the rights of men.

The Necessity and Divine Origin of Authority: ¶46–¶52

The Pope's understanding of authority has its roots in two thousand years of Church history, during which Church-state relationships have been good and bad. Authority is good because men, being social by nature, need to have their rights coordinated, protected, and promoted. The Holy Father rejects those theories which regard governmental and political authority as something sinister and at best a necessary evil. Authority can *become* evil and tyrannical, but this is a deviation, a corruption of something which is good when it operates within the limits of the moral law. Authority is not a social convention or contract in the Rousseau sense of the word; it originates in the moral order and is a necessary element in any human society. But it must always function within the framework of its essential mission, the promotion and protection of the rights of man, ensuring them by what modern society calls civil rights legislation.

Authority is a coordinating element, not a substitute for the initiative of the private citizen. Authority seeks to promote free obedience to the good, and when it constantly applies force and threats to make men keep the laws or do the good, a truly human society no longer exists. Conversely, if the authority commands something which is against the moral law, the binding force of that authority is lost.

How does the Pope derive his concept of authority? Since authority is an influence on the human person, on a conscious and free being, it is an influence which must be specifically human, that is, which must coincide with man's specific nature. Kant's theory that authority is the ability to constrain is not true because constraint is not a specifically human influence. Authority must address itself to intelligence and free will because man acts from his interiority, which is conscious and free. But since an integral part of man is his body, authority will also have to influence man's activity. In any *human* action, man's knowledge and free will posit the action to perform and the reasons for performing that particular action. It follows, then, that if authority addresses itself to intelligence and free will, it is an influence on the acts of man.

Man's supreme good is God, and his total and ultimate end is a correct attitude toward God; in Christianity this attitude, which must permeate all human action, is that of charity. And since all ends are subordinate to this ultimate end, the influence of this end constitutes the supreme and as it were the only authority, for all is directed to God. Within their proper domains, the demands of a particular and subordinate end constitute authority insofar as they depend on this end. In this sense, all correct authority comes from God.

As St. Thomas teaches, man's intelligence is the first organ of authority because it directs action through its knowledge of the moral end to be accomplished and the means to accomplish it. "In the first place a man's nature is subjected to the order of his own reason."[2] For man's intelligence to understand the demands of the end, however, he must be aided by prudence: "Prudence makes a man well disposed in regard to things that are to be chosen for the sake of the end."[3] St. Thomas continues:

Through this possession of the capacity to exercise providence [by intelligence and prudence], one may also direct and govern his own acts. Thus, the rational creature participates in divine providence, not only by being governed passively, but also by governing actively, for he governs himself in his personal acts and even others.[4]

The organ of authority is needed to reach a desired end. Far from arbitrary, this authority conforms to a particular end to be achieved in the moral sphere. For example, a law of education

[2]*Summa Theologica*, I–II, q. 87, art. 1.
[3]*Summa contra Gentiles*, III, chap. 35.
[4]*Ibid.*, chap. 113.

demands that children go to school until they have reached their sixteenth birthday. This moral demand prepares the citizen to live properly in a democratic and technological society such as ours. Those who realize this do not need a law; they would spontaneously send their children to school until well over that age. Yet there are a few who do not see this demand of the common good, and authority is used to coerce them. The government *is* not authority, but it *has* authority; it has authority because individual men cannot be knowledgeable about all things. If an individual breaks his leg, he knows that the healing of his leg is the end to be accomplished, but he does not know the means. He therefore submits to a doctor in obedience; he submits to an exterior authority who has the means to accomplish the end. The doctor *has* authority and is consequently an organ of authority. This same principle applies to the authority of the state.

The economic, cultural, political, and intellectual orders are very complicated in contemporary society, and authority must attempt a general regulation of these areas for the good of all. No individual man is capable of understanding the operations and ramifications of all these complicated orders, and he therefore cannot be his own authority. When man submits himself to another because he is incapable, the submission is called *law*: "Law is the rule and measure of acts in reason, which is the first principle of human acts."[5] The head of a state and its lawmakers must act out of prudence, not for themselves but for others. St. Thomas calls this "architectonic prudence." The lawmaker acts as an architect by directing the actions of all citizens toward the soundest total good.

The human person is thus a dynamic being who must attain

[5]*Summa Theologica,* I–II, q. 90, art. 1.

certain ends. The influence of these ends constitutes his authority. A person has authority inasmuch as he is a mediator between people and the exigencies of the ends which these people must attain. In other words, every organ of authority is at the service of others; it serves the exigencies of the end which men will or must realize. That is why heads of government are called ministers. Christ gave the perfect definition of authority when He said, "I have not come to be ministered unto, but to minister. Whoever wished to be first among you must be the servants of all" (Mk 10:44–45). The pope is called the servant of the servants of God. The priest has his ministry, the government has its ministers, and all institutions have their administrators.

The man with authority must have a double love, a love for the end and a love for the person or persons he must direct to that end. The end determines the competence and limits of authority, and the persons who are to attain this end determine the amount of authority which must be used. But persons under authority must act on their own initiative. The organ of authority must never crush this personal initiative; it is always to be in the service of this initiative. There are therefore certain principles which the organ of authority should remember: it must respect the personal initiative of others; it must supplement initiative when necessary; it must orient initiative when it deviates from the right course; and it must use force if necessary, but only as a last resort. All this the Holy Father explains in detail.

He who exercises authority is therefore the mediator between a person or a community of persons and the end which this person or community wishes to or must realize. In order to study closely the content (object, extension, limits) of this mediation, Pope John later considers the exercise of authority, which will be considered in the order of social life and in the context of the state. As his immediate topic of discussion, however, the Holy Father next considers the purpose for the existence of public authority and the essentials of the common good.

Attainment of the Common Good Is the Purpose of the Public Authority; and Essentials of the Common Good: ¶53–¶59

Authority, which exists to promote and safeguard the rights of the human person, is a necessary element of any community because interrelationships are complicated and need coordination. In other words, authority is needed to ensure the good of all citizens because of the complicated nature of any particular society, and because of the selfishness and laziness of some citizens who are interested only in themselves. This is noteworthy, for the power of wealth has often been used to exploit many citizens of a country; the poor are at a great disadvantage without resources. For these reasons, then, a lawful authority is needed to promote an impartial social justice in the community. From this point of view, the public authority protects the rights of all its citizens by promoting the common good.

The Holy Father is realistic: he recognizes and insists that the common good is economic, social, and cultural. Any effective social order must take into consideration the fact that man is an incarnate spirit, composed both of body and soul. The Holy Father's encyclical *Mater et Magistra* is directed toward this aspect of social justice. All that is necessary for the discussion here are some fundamental considerations on the notion of the common good and what the common good entails.

St. Thomas says that the essence of a community is the suitable disposition of many toward one end. This disposition consists in many persons' living and working together to promote individual and general well-being, but a necessary corollary to this is that these persons also promote the subjective culture or development of each member. Some fifty years ago, authors spoke of objective culture and the task of each community member to increase objective culture. These authors went no farther: they completely neglected the fact that objective culture exists for the subjective culture of each member of the community. Since man becomes richer through his relations with external realities, he must be open to the realities of the world. Therefore, it is only in living the meaning of his relations to the world that man can perfect himself. The total end of man is that he work in union with others to promote objective culture, which allows the growth of subjective culture. This total end must be achieved before man can accomplish his partial end, his own subjective culture. St. Thomas saw this when he said that the individual is to society as the part is to the whole. The part is directed to the whole, and as a result, the part profits the whole.

Since the individual (the part) is in an integral relation to society (the whole), a consideration of the proper structure of this integral relationship or, as it has been called previously, the *common good* is in order. The common good can be examined in at least four ways: the internal end, the immediate end, the ulterior end, and the means.

First, because persons in a society live together, the common good can be studied as the *internal* end. The health of a person is an intrinsic good. There is also the health of a group, that is, the group's equilibrium, which depends on a material element and a formal element. The material element needed for the common good is that the community be comprised of many members, each with his own diversity and originality. Each member must be allowed the free development of his own originality. This places responsibility on both the person and society: the person has the responsibility developing his tendencies, capacities, talents, and so forth; society must ensure favorable conditions for each member to develop his originality. But since the acceptance of responsibility by the person and by society is a free act, liberty is primary.

The formal element needed for the common good is love. Diversity is ambiguous; it can be the source of disparity or of unity. Love and all the virtues in its service must be present to achieve the common good. Again, this presents a responsibility to the person and to society. The person has the responsibility of developing and cultivating this love. Society, on the other hand, has the responsibility of promoting the community's morality, made up of all the virtues which pertain to the social life, of which, however, liberty comes first.

The common good can be considered as the *immediate* end, that is, mutual cooperation in the community to realize objective culture. The immediate end can take different forms: in a complete society, the form has as its end the realization of all the objective values needed for man to live in society; in an incomplete society, the form has as its end the realization of certain objective values. In either form, however, each person must cooperate in the achievement of objective culture according to his capabilities. That means that he must work in his particular profession or specialty. When Marx, Engels, and Lenin said that each must work according to his capacities, they were expressing a Christian concept. Each man has a social obligation to contribute to the common good. Even if someone has enough money so that he does not have to work for himself, he still has the duty of contributing to the common good.

84

However, this duty applies only to those who are capable of working; children, old people, and the sick, for instance, cannot be expected to work. This fact brings out a point which is often forgotten. The community could not subsist if those who could work did not work for the good of all. Those who are capable of working must provide a sufficient objective culture for the other members of the community. The reciprocity of giving and receiving the benefits of cooperation is a common reality in our existence. The best example of this is the family. In their early years, children receive everything from their parents. As they grow older, they begin to work, and then they aid their parents, who by that time are perhaps unable to work. But to repeat, liberty is again of primary importance. Cooperation is not instinctive; man must freely agree to contribute his part in this collaboration.

The common good can also be considered as the *ulterior end,* in which the subjective culture of every individual is realized. As mentioned above, only people who are capable can work together for objective culture, and they can only do this for a certain length of time (they grow old, get sick, retire, and so on). Yet the subjective culture of each person must be achieved. Therefore, the ulterior end of the common good is that objective culture be directed to the achievement of the subjective culture of all. Marx and Engels saw this when they said that each should receive according to his needs. It may seem strange that the individual's end is the subjective culture of all, but it is only by promoting this general good that he can achieve his individual good. Again, liberty is the determining factor; the accomplishment of this ulterior end depends upon attitudes which man can take if he wishes to. He is always free. For example, a university can be the finest in the world, have the best professors and a good library, and so forth, but without the free choice of the student to take advantage of his opportunity, all these things are useless to him.

The common good can be considered under a fourth aspect, the *means* for its achievement, which calls for a certain kind of organization. The word *organization* derives from the Greek word *organon,* instrument. Organization is simply the means for assuring the realization of the three aspects of the common good which have been discussed. Therefore, there should be an organ of authority, laws, precepts, institutions, and all other necessary means to achieve the common good.

If the virtue of love—and hence of justice—was perfect among men, an organization would probably not be needed. Love would assure men's cooperation for the development of objective culture, which in time would be directed to the subjective culture of each member of society. Justice would assure that the relations between the people living together were correct (communitive justice), that these people would cooperate for the sake of objective culture (legal justice), and that this objective culture would be directed toward the subjective culture of each member (distributive justice). This view is hypothetical, however, because real men are not perfect. Organization exists so that the imperfection of man does not prevent members of a community from living together, from cooperating in objective culture, and frome achieving subjective culture.

Organization is necessary because of man's ignorance and egoism. Organization must ensure that all of the requisites are nonetheless fulfilled. There are few people who know all the social duties which are required in a society; furthermore, man has a tendency to think only of himself. Organization is needed for unity of action, because a certain unity in economy, in law, in common defense, and so on is necessary to man's well-being.

Ultimately, then, laws, precepts, institutions, and other means are needed to offset man's imperfections. St. Thomas speaks of laws as being necessary for man because of the infirmity caused by original sin. However, he also says that authority would exist even if there were no sin for at least one reason. Each man has his own task to fulfill in society. He must occupy himself with this task. His task will determine his perspective, his own particular view. There must be something to keep all these different points of view unified, and that will be the organization in society.

Because the most important responsibility of the public authority is to promote the common good, the Holy Father's discussion moves to a specific consideration of the relationship between the public authority and the common good. And since the end of all public authority is to promote and protect individual rights, its involvement with the common good will be characterized by the degree to which it allows the free function of these rights.

Responsibilities of the Public Authority, and the Rights and Duties of Individuals; and Reconciliation and Protection of the Rights of Individuals: ¶60–¶62

The Holy Father's comments in the encyclical are noteworthy because they are neither so general as to be platitudes nor so specific as to be doctrinaire. Above all, he insists on this principle: the promotion, protection, and coordination of human rights by public authority. Much room is left for the public authority to deliberate and decide upon its own competence, which is determined by the stage of cultural and economic development of the society that it governs. The directives are general enough to provide for any contingencies that might arise in the future.

The Holy Father does not deal with an ideal Platonic community. His message is to an imperfect world which is filled with injustice and in which all men of good will are called to work. To the public authority in places where rights have been denied, he insists that it has a moral obligation to restore them without delay. As the first part of the encyclical puts it, any government is a tyranny to the extent that it does not seek this end with impartiality.

Since authority is a human influence on man, it is an appeal to his free and conscious efforts to attain the rational and therefore moral end of the common good. In this sense, one of the essential roles of the political and socal authority is to guarantee and actively promote civil rights and liberties by law. In the light of these social teachings of the Holy Father, it is difficult to see how any Catholic, or any man of good will for that matter, can oppose sane promotion of civil liberties; in fact, the Pope encourages Catholics to take an active part in the attainment and promotion of civil liberties for all members of the community. The Holy Father is realistic here: history clearly demonstrates that when the individual citizens of a country do not make it their solemn duty to promote the human rights of all citizens, terrible abuses and even political tyranny result. A true democracy can only be the fruit of eternal vigilance and effort.

Yet while the rights of men are absolute, their practical exercise is limited. Every human liberty is limited by the simple fact that it is an incarnate liberty. The public authority has the practical problem of deciding the limits to the exercise of rights for the harmonious interaction and common welfare of all citizens. These limits are both internal and external.

Internal limits can come from a man's free will, which chooses whether or not to exercise a right. While the right to an education always exists for the individual, it may be that he never exercises the right, thus relinquishing it through omission. Rights can also be abused. Many landholders, even today, abuse the right of ownership by opposing an equitable use of the land. Because a few of the wealthy possess much of the land, the many are slaves and cannot exercise the superior right of usage. The state must see to it that the rights of some members of the community do not impede the equal rights of other members. Since man is limited in his capabilities, it constitutes as great an injustice for a person to attempt more that he is able as for him not to do as much as his capabilities permit out of laziness. The ideal state exists when each person exercises his rights according to his capabilities. Thus, political authority must guarantee that all members of the community use their rights according to their capabilities by fostering and creating the proper conditions. The reason for this is exposed later in what Pope John and others have called the principle of subsidiarity.

External limits arise from the rights of others, which the individual and the public authority must take into consideration. An individual cannot exercise a right at the expense of an equal or superior right of another. Since rights can be abused, authority must regulate the correct exercise of rights. (A person has the right, for instance, to use the highway since he has the right of communication. That right, however, does not mean that he can drive in any way he wishes, because the rights of others are concerned. The public authority must establish traffic regulations which must be obeyed.) In any given society there are also material conditions which limit rights. A person has the right to work, but its exercise is limited in a period of recession when it it difficult to find employment. In such a case, external realities in the form of economic conditions determine the exercise of a right. Owing to industrial and economic progress, however, man is able to exercise more of his rights more often. The limits to rights which depend on material conditions change with the progress of culture; these limits continually demand analysis and adequate reform to facilitate the greatest possible exercise of rights, an activity proper to the public authority.

The task is difficult and complex, and that is why the Holy Father gives no rigid blueprint to any particular society. The objective possibilities for the full exercise of human rights will vary from one community to another.

The Duty of Promoting the Rights of Individuals: ¶63–¶64

Man is a material being; therefore, he has basic economic needs to which he is entitled in justice. The state must protect and safeguard him in this respect, for man cannot live in dignity and peace without the assurance of a basic substratum of material goods. From this flows the right to unemployment insurance, the right to work, to health, to life, and all other rights which enhance his incarnate existence. Workers must also share in the responsibility of their work, for they are not mere cogs in a vast production machine. Shared profits, stockholdings in the company, and so on are all practical ways of ensuring worker responsibility. In ¶64, the Holy Father outlines simply what he has treated exhaustively in his earlier encyclical *Mater et Magistra*. Readers are referred to that letter for a fuller discussion of this concept.

As the Holy Father implies, man is not simply a *Homo œconomicus* and *Homo faber;* he is also *Homo rationalis, Homo sapiens.* Because man is also spirit, he has nonmaterial values. He has the right to aesthetic, intellectual, and other cultural values. If man is to be benefited in the totality of his being, the authority must therefore also promote, by itself or through private groups, rights which are not material. The right of education is especially important, for it is the principal means whereby men foster their various tendencies and abilities. The authority may establish educational laws and standards and subsidize various cultural endeavors, as in the fields of music and painting. Out of respect for private initiative, the promotion of these values is to be reserved to private groups whenever possible, but when private promotion fails or is insufficient for the general good, public authority has the right to ensure effective promotion. In this way, the objective culture of any particular community is enriched and is further directed to the subjective perfection of each citizen.

Though it is very important to the common good for the objective wealth of any society to be equitably distributed, the Christian's ultimate concern for material objects can never be a pure materialism, even when modified by a species of subjective perfection. He must always direct his efforts toward specifically Christian values. When God created the universe, He looked on it and found it good, and He gave man dominion over this good. This material offered to man in farm and factory should be used to create a community in which no one need starve or go naked. Man should put matter to work for the greater good of his neighbors, who are all of mankind. Christ commanded His followers to feed the hungry and heal the sick: "Inasmuch as you have done it for one of the least of these, my brethren, you have done it for me" (Mt 25:40). Because Christ gave His blessing to material things, the Christian's dedication to them must be for His reasons.

From his discussion of the relationship that exists between the public authority and the common good, the Holy Father proceeds in the next two paragraphs to the principles that should always guide the public authority in any intervention that it makes for the common good. Again, the overriding concern must be the establishment of the conditions necessary to the free expression of human rights.

Harmonizing the Two Forms of Intervention by the Public Authority: ¶65–¶66

Too much government tends to crush the initiative of private citizens and groups; too little government may encourage abuse in the community. To keep a proper balance between these two extremes is often a difficult task. Yet whatever solution is attempted (and this will vary in different times and places), the principle of *subsidiarity* must always be respected.

Papal teaching has often stressed the principle of subsidiarity. What does it mean? In general, each person's destiny consists in the objective meaning of his relationships and the realization of what he is in himself. He must develop the original talents which God has confined to him. To attain his full capabilities, the person must freely initiate the development of his potentialities.

In *Quadragesimo anno,* Pope Pius XI capsulized the principle of subsidiarity: the unchangeable and eternal principle of social philosophy is that a society may not appropriate to itself the initiative which can be assumed by the individual. The fundamental reason for this lies in the irreplaceable value of a person's free initiative in directing his destiny. Since each person must fulfill his own destiny through his own genius, he must be able to take advantage of all the means necessary to develop it. The function of the public authority will be simply to create favorable conditions for this development.

There is also a social reason for subsidiarity: the riches and fruitfulness of society come from the diversity of its members; but this diversity is obviously related to how each person develops his individual talents by free initiative. The fullest exercise of human rights occurs when the will keeps pace with ability and when ability is confined by nothing but personal limitations. As this diversity is allowed to develop, society is enriched. Obviously, then, the society that permits and encourages its members to perfect their potential perfects itself.

The Structure and Operation of the Public Authority; and Law and Conscience: ¶67–¶72

As stated several times above, it is impossible to set one political and social pattern for every time and circumstance. Societies are uneven in their economic, social, and cultural development, and the stage of development in each area must be taken into consideration by its public authority. In a highly industrialized society, for example, cultural advantages will be more available to the citizen than in a rural or backward society.

Significantly, however, the Holy Father praises the threefold division of power in the political order: "We consider, however, that it is in keeping with the innate demands of human nature that the state should take a form which embodies the threefold division of powers corresponding to the three principal functions of public authority" (¶ 68). To the author's knowledge, this is the first time that praise like this has been incorporated in a Church document as authoritative as an encyclical. However, Pope John was not the first supreme pontiff to endorse constitutional and democratic government; Pius XII boldly spoke out in its defense many times. In his Christmas Message of 1944, Pius XII said that in a true democracy,

. . . the citizen feels with him the consciousness of his personality, of his duties and rights, of his own freedom joined to respect for the freedom and dignity of others . . . to express his own views of the duties and sacrifices that are imposed on him, [and] not [to be] compelled to obey without being heard; these are two rights of the citizen which find in democracy, as its name implies, their expression. . . . If, then, we consider the extent and nature of the sacrifices demanded of all citizens, especially in our day when the activity of the state is so vast and decisive, the democratic form of government appears to many as a postulate of nature imposed by reason itself.[6]

This statement is perhaps the strongest endorsement of any type of government to be found in papal literature. Pius XII's definite preference for the principles of democratic government is noteworthy, because it has always been the contention of the Church that human dignity and rights could be safeguarded in a variety of governmental forms. In *Pacem in terris,* John XXIII is equally forceful in his preference for the modern forms of democratic procedure:

[6]Pius XII's radio broadcast on Christmas Eve, 1944, as quoted in Vincent A. Yzermans, ed., *The Major Addresses of Pope Pius XII,* II (St. Paul, 1961), p. 81.

It must not be concluded, however, because authority comes from God, that therefore men have no right to choose those who are to rule the state, to decide the form of government, and to determine both the way in which authority is to be exercised and its limits. It is thus clear that the doctrine which We have set forth is fully consonant with any truly democratic regime [¶ 52].

The democratic form of government, then, is explicitly approved by both Pius XII and John XXIII, but it is equally clear that both pontiffs are speaking of truly democratic governments, and not the counterfeit shams that exist behind the Iron Curtain.

By endorsing democratic forms of government, Pope John once again expresses his acceptance of the modern world. The three-fold division of governmental powers—legislature, executive, and judicial—is a modern development dating from the eighteenth century, that found its expression in France in Montesquieu and earlier in the English tradition of constitutional law. Although the formation of this concept goes back at least to John of Salisbury (d. 1180), its practical implementation has not occurred until fairly recently. In the democratic concept, the limits of the public authority are generally written into laws, constitutions, bills of rights, and other public documents to ensure the rights of all the citizens more effectively. Pope John mentions this procedure, which has become one of the hallmarks of the democratic process.

> . . . it is required that the constitution of each political community be formulated in proper legal terminology, and that there be defined therein the manner in which the state authorities are to be designated, how their mutual relations are to be regulated, what are to be their spheres of competence, and finally, the forms and systems they are obliged to follow in the performance of their office [¶ 76].

Officials and ministers of government are not to overstep the bounds set by these limiting ordinances. If the ruler does overstep these limits, he incurs the ultimate anathema that the modern democratic community places on its rulers: unconstitutionality. In the division of power, the Holy Father sees a protection against abuses by public officials and a surer guarantee of the rights of citizens. In the Western tradition of democratic government, each division acts as a check and a balance to the others, thus preventing any one division from usurping complete power.

In short, democracy is the exercise of political authority which derives its "just powers from the consent of the governed" and which is accountable to the governed, who are ultimately sovereign. The consensus of the people is thus the source of government's legitimacy. And in the government "of the people, by the people, for the people," this consensus must be the result of free and public discussion, not coercion and violence. Democracy does not demand a vulgar egalitarianism, but it does demand that all citizens, from the president of the country down to the modest laborer, be equal before the law, enjoy equal protection under the law, and not be deprived of any of their rights without due process of law.

In a true democracy, all men are also equal in the enjoyment of their rights. If certain men hold opinions contrary to or different from those of the majority, it is incumbent on a democratic community to respect and tolerate the expression of these opinions as long as they are in no way criminal. When differing opinions are to be adjudged with regard to the common good, a true democracy recognizes the supreme law of the land as the juridical norm for decision. That is, a constitution, a bill of rights, or some other such public document that is true and binding for every citizen is accepted as the final arbiter for diverse points of view.

Regardless of the structure of the public authority, the rights of citizens must be guaranteed by civil law, which has its basis in natural law. This basis is evident when it is understood that natural law recognizes man as the subject of rights. Man is a moral being because he is conscious and free and thus independent and responsible; this is the dignity of the human person, which must be respected, and this dignity is the source of all his rights. Natural law is not a restriction but rather a recognition of man's liberty and thus of his dignity and his rights.

Although natural law is unchangeable, the Christian tradition has recognized that man's knowledge of natural law can change, and particularly can become more specified. In this sense, natural law is not some ever-present sameness, reconfirmed by each generation; it is dynamic and open. But is there progress regarding the content of natural law? As shown previously, the content of natural law is the objective meaning of a person's being. In man's perception of the content of natural law progress is possible, since the content is the ideal never to be fulfilled but always to be sought.

The content of natural law is realized to a greater degree as man's internal awareness expands. He can be educated to know more completely the content of the natural law; that is to say, he will have an increasing realization of all that is human, and through this he will come to see more clearly in what the content of natural law consists. For instance, polygamy realizes a part of the natural law. It assures procreation and a certain type of education. This education, however, is incomplete because it perpetuates a situation in which women are not equal to men, thus making the idea of love incomplete. By education, man is led to the state of monogamy through a fuller understanding of natural law; in this state of love, procreation and education are better realized. Thus, the content of natural law is dynamic in the sense that the ideal is realized to the degree that the dignity of the human person is recognized. As man's knowledge of and esteem for humans progress, his objective understanding of their being progresses.

The external conditions, the material possibilities of a society have a bearing on man's understanding of the natural law. Nowadays, for example, the question of education is posed in a different way. In times past, if a child was not needed to help support the family, he could go to school and obtain an education. Now, however, most people insist that the child has received his possibilities and capabilities from God, and that to develop them he must be educated. The reason for the greater achievement of this ideal is the improvement of economic conditions.

Improvements in internal and external conditions, then, bring about changes in understanding that demonstrate the dynamism in the natural law. Positive civil law is also related to this progress in natural law. Civil law is defined as the rule of life according to the demands of the common good; it consists of laws imposed for the good of the state. In brief, civil law is the rule of social life. Since natural law is the objective meaning of man's being, the state, when it imposes a law, must take this into account. Thus, the relationship between civil law and natural law is intrinsic. Several consequences follow from this relationship.

The first consequence is stated by St. Thomas[7] when he says

[7] See *Summa Theologica,* I–II, q. 95, art. 1, and q. 96, arts. 4 and 6.

that civil laws are derived from natural law. Natural law, then, is concretized in a civil law that arises from certain historic circumstances. Through knowledge, for example, certain conclusions are drawn from natural law, and these become the law of the people (*ius gentium*). Yet laws are derived from natural law prudently; even if all of natural law were known, its full content could not be applied to certain societies. The historic circumstances of the people of a given society must be considered; they must be educated and slowly brought closer to the ideal set forth by natural law.

The second consequence derived from the intrinsic relationship between natural and positive law is that positive law binds in conscience. St. Thomas has said that if certain laws are just, they bind in conscience because of natural law, from which they are derived.

This obligation leads directly to a third consequence: the purpose of positive law is to assure the moral education of its citizens. Slowly but surely, the state should bring its citizens to a closer realization of the ideal of the moral law. Again, however, prudence must always prevail. If the state tries to impose a law containing many moral implications for which the people are not ready, it can do more harm than good. In the United States, an outstanding example of premature legislation was prohibition.

Finally, positive law is increasingly completed and renovated by natural law. Every positive law is a particular concretization of some aspect of natural law. There are always imperfections in positive law, but as men come to a greater realization of the dignity of man, these imperfections will be corrected by new laws, which will be derived from a more accurate understanding of natural law. At a certain time in history, for example, nations abolished slavery, thus incorporating a greater recognition of man's dignity, an ideal of natural law, into positive law.

The intrinsic relationship between civil and natural law, however, does not mean that the two are identical; though they are not completely separate, they are still distinct. Natural law obliges in conscience, but if man does not wish to conform to natural law, he cannot be forced. The obligation to obey is a moral one. On the other hand, civil authorities can inflict punishment if civil law is not obeyed; force can be applied in order to guarantee that man conforms.

Furthermore, the nature of civil law is not the same as that of natural law. Since positive law is human, an act of man, it is imperfect and limited. This human limitation makes positive law relative and not universal; St. Thomas states, "Legislators in framing laws attend to what commonly happens."[8] Natural law, however, is based on the objective meaning of man's being and is therefore universal. But the relative nature of positive law does not mean that it does not bind in conscience; it does mean that the law binds in many things, not in all. There can be exceptions to the law.

St. Thomas refers to this when he speaks of *epikeia* or *aequitas* (equity), the superior form of legal justice.[9] He means by this that a law can be observed by the letter or by the spirit. By observing the letter of the law, the individual simply limits himself to the literal prescriptions of the law in all circumstances; by obeying the spirit of the law, the individual observes its true sense.

The idea of *epikeia* arises from the spirit of the law. In this superior form, positive law is always considered in relation to

[8]*Ibid.*, II–II, q. 120, art. 1.
[9]*Ibid.*, art. 2.

2394 1

natural law. The mother of an infant, for instance, knows that she must attend mass on Sunday, a positive law, but she also knows that according to natural law she must take care of her child. By disregarding the positive law of mass attendance, she obeys the dictates of natural law. Sometimes more is demanded than what positive law prescribes. For example, the law of abstinence on certain days is a form of mortification required by positive law, but if abstinence is not a form of mortification for an individual, he must do more than the positive law demands. Thus, in certain cases, *epikeia* prescribes a violation of the letter of the law in order that the spirit of the law be kept; in other cases, more must be done than the law prescribes. These exceptions hold only for positive law, which is relative; there are no exceptions to natural law, which is universal and unchangeable.

Another important distinction between positive and natural law is the form in which they address themselves to individuals. Positive law is an exterior prescription which is imposed. The legislator cannot penetrate man's interiority. For example, he can impose taxes on individuals, but he cannot make them like taxes. Natural law, on the contrary, is interior; it addresses itself to the will. The interior decision determines the morality of the act. If circumstances prevent an act of adultery, for instance, the person who desires the act is still an adulterer. "But I say to you that anyone who so much as looks with lust at a woman has already committed adultery with her in his heart" (Mt 5:28). The interior conviction is the source of the exterior act. This is an illustration of the weakness of positive law and the strength of natural law.

Moreover, the viewpoint of positive law is different from that of natural law. Natural law prescribes something because it is good or it prohibits something because it is evil. The viewpoint of natural law, therefore, is moral. The viewpoint of the positive law is social; it is concerned with the common good of the community.

This social viewpoint gives rise to certain consequences. Because of its intrinsic relation to natural law, positive law can never prescribe what is morally evil, but it does not have to prohibit all that is morally evil. In places which are not fully civilized, for example, legislators must tolerate much that is contrary to natural law until the people are morally educated. This accounts for the fact that there are different systems of legislation, for legislation depends on the historic circumstances of a people, their traditions, and their culture. It cannot be said *a priori* that one system is better than another. The concrete content of the common good of one people will differ from that of another, and legislation must begin in this concrete reality; but simultaneously it must push toward a closer realization of the natural law. The legislator has a difficult task. He must know the community, and he must know sociology. He must be a virtuous man, intellectually as well as morally.

To summarize briefly, natural law is the internal norm of liberty. It is universal and absolute, an ideal which is to be pursued. Positive law is the extrinsic norm of liberty because it is given by a legislator who is exterior to the governed, it directs external actions, and it can impose external force. But positive human laws do bind in conscience because of the intrinsic relationship between civil law and natural law. The whole question of whether or not civil law binds in conscience depends on what is stressed. If the emphasis is on the relationship with natural law, then civil laws bind in conscience; if it is on the distinction between positive law and natural law, the distinction may be so great that certain civil laws will be reduced to mere penal measures that do not bind in conscience. An understanding of these distinctions is important when determining the extent to which positive civil law should apply in concrete situations.

The form of the public authority cannot be determined once and for all, but the very nature of man indicates that he can participate in self-government. Pope John's discussion of the public authority continues with a consideration of citizens' participation in public life.

Citizens' Participation in Public Life: ¶73–¶74

In certain societies, the objective culture is richer and more advanced than in others; consequently, it permits citizens a more varied and fuller participation in its economic and cultural benefits. The duty of the public authority is to allow each citizen to participate in the riches of the objective culture in proportion to his capacities. This might be called a pedagogic duty of the state. The function of legislation, in this regard, is to guarantee the proper use by all citizens of the economic, cultural, and social resources within the community. To this end, the state must encourage the citizen to participate in self-government, not only because the citizen has a right to do so, but also because the enrichment of society demands it. The need for participation is obvious in modern technological societies where, by and large, hunger and poverty no longer rule men's lives and where the citizens now have the time, leisure, and education to participate intelligently. There is a rewarding interdependency here: technology allows men the leisure to pursue education which in turn is employed in technology.

103

There are laws which annoy only those who are incapable of keeping them. This is so, for instance, when a law is enacted to repair an omission of duty. When the cultural level of a country requires a certain degree of intellectual formation and when the economic conditions are favorable, the authority of the state can introduce the obligation for all citizens to attend school until a certain age. The authority substitutes itself for the parents, who have the duty and the right to educate their children. This function is legitimate because it protects the parents against their own negligence; the state would go too far, however, if it did not allow the parents the liberty of choosing the school which they think gives the guarantee of extending family education. Since legal obligation is necessary only when parents are remiss in their duties, however, there must be as much liberty as possible in this domain.

Substitutive functions are also valid when economic and social progress permit the public authority to protect the community against great risks and burdens for which most people are unprepared. The state can impose laws concerning social security. It can even make insurance obligatory, if this is necessary as a protection against dangerous negligence. But again, the personal initiative of each person must be respected; for example, in the choice of the insurance preferred. As much liberty as possible must be allowed. As the Holy Father constantly stresses in the encyclical, the end of all regulation and law is not restraint but freedom, for truly, freedom defines the human person.

Like Part I, Part II concludes with an examination of contemporary society. Here Pope John is concerned specifically with modern man's tendencies in the domain of public authority.

Characteristics of the Present Day: ¶75-¶79

The final paragraphs sum up the thoughts Pope John has repeated throughout Part II of the encyclical. Laws are for the protection of men's rights, and modern men seem to feel more secure when these rights as well as the obligations and duties of officials are written into constitutions and other public documents.

In modern democracies, at least in theory, no one, not even the public authority, is above the law or the constitution. All are equal before the law, which is administered impartially to everyone, from the richest to the poorest and the strongest to the weakest. To quote a famous American jurist, "The law is colorblind." As stated in the Declaration of Independence: "We hold these truths to be self-evident, that all men are created equal, that they are endowed by their Creator with certain inalienable rights ... that to secure these rights, governments are instituted among men ..." This American document is a perfect reflection of the Holy Father's meaning: the essential duty of the organ of authority is to promote the common good, thereby assuring and protecting the rights of its citizens.

St. Thomas captured this concept in one short phrase: *principis est ordinare*—it is the duty of the ruler to direct. For him, the word *direct* always referred to finality, the disposition of many and diverse things toward one end. This definition must be considered in a social context where the common good is the end in view; hence, the organ of authority must intervene so that the different members of the community attain to the common good.

Authority is necessary to the community. Since the end would not be achieved without it, the exercise of authority belongs essentially to the community. This follows from the definition of a

105

community: a unity of order directed toward a certain end. The very sense of a community implies an exercise of authority.

To exercise this authority, however, the community needs the proper means. As a man needs the organ of his eye to see, so the community needs an organ to exercise authority. Individual members of a society do not usually have the competence required to grasp the exigencies of cooperation in social and cultural goods; in addition, many do not have the generosity needed to work for the perfection of all. Therefore, authority must compensate for both ignorance and egoism. Furthermore, since men have their own opinions, they will choose different ends and different means, thus disrupting unity. In this case, authority must be the stabilizing element. Yet there is a more important reason for the existence of an organ of authority. Insofar as the individual exercises his rightful activities or profession, his particular end, he realizes objective culture, and thereby indirectly enriches the common good; an organ of authority is needed because it *formally* and *directly* intends the common good.

The state must be considered the framework within which the community cooperates for the common good. To ensure this cooperation, the state may impose necessary sacrifices on the community. It may levy taxes to maintain its administration, courts, and all other public institutions and structures; it may nationalize and socialize through the right of eminent domain when this is needed for the common good, as in the case of the St. Lawrence Seaway. In all of these actions, however, the state must scrupulously respect the principle of subsidiarity.

Because it is an organization, the state is in the service of the social life of the community; that is, the legislative and administrative functions, the institutions, and the organs of the state are only means which are relative to the demands of the common good. Consequently, the organization of the state has a double aspect. First, organization changes as social life evolves. As the objective culture of the community grows, the organization must adapt itself accordingly. And as the people make further progress in subjective culture, they become more aware of their personal initiative and need to participate more fully in the exercise of power in the community. Second, however, a certain stability must always remain in organization. Life must continue, and any complete change in organization can disrupt the well-being of the community. Changes in the organization must be adapted to the needs of the community's social life, but of these needs, stability is paramount.

But the state remains always a means. The end of any human society is liberty, which is attained by justice, a quality in turn based on respect for the truth of the moral law and the sacredness of the rights of man. The effort to achieve liberty is animated and realized through the virtue of love. This dynamic and human concept of the social order was eminently that of John XXIII.

Part III

Relations Between States

PART III of the encyclical *Pacem in terris* also examines the rights of persons, but at the higher level of relationships between states. Racism in all its forms is condemned for the reason that "All men are equal in their natural dignity. Consequently . . . all communities are of equal natural dignity, since they are bodies whose membership is made up of these same human beings" (¶ 89). The foundation of the familial, social, and political community, namely, the inviolate rights and duties of the human person, is also at the basis of relationships between states: "For the same natural law which governs relations between individual human beings must also regulate the relations of political communities with one another" (¶ 80). International problems must be resolved not by the economic or military strength of any political community but by the moral law which rules nations as well as individuals.

Since the internal juridical order of a state is concerned with relations among individuals, the first principle which must regulate the functioning of this order is respect for the human person. In the same way, the first principle in the international juridical order is respect for the equal rights of individual nations, especially their right to self-determination. Insofar as international relations affect individual persons, actually or potentially, it is in their interest that this principle be respected. But international law must also be able to limit the discretionary power of a state over its own nationals; and this limiting power derives from the natural law. The criminal excesses of Nazi rule have unambiguously demanded that natural law prevail in the international juridical order.

Since World War II, there have been many successful attempts to transpose the principles of natural law into the field of positive law. In the effort to ensure adequate protection for fundamental human rights and freedoms, for example, precepts of natural law have been formulated in the Convention on Genocide and the famous Universal Declaration of the Rights of Man. In Western Europe, the European Convention for the Protection of Human Rights and Fundamental Freedoms, now in force, constitutes a positive law of great value and extensive application. A glance at the impressive list of conventions concluded in the fields of labor and social security dispels any doubt as to the universal applicability of natural law. The degree to which so many of the principles of natural law have been embodied in international law indicates how fundamental these principles are in the relations that are to prevail among states. The Holy Father analyzes these relations in Part III of *Pacem in terris*.

Subjects of Rights and Duties: ¶80–¶85

In the opening paragraphs of Part III, Pope John again says that in the dealings of one nation with others, what matters is not size, economic wealth, or power but rather adherence to moral law. It is most difficult for nations—especially large and powerful ones—to realize that there is a rule of order, of basic morality, which supersedes power politics. The law among nations is much more than the summation of individual greeds which prompt one nation to exploit other nations whenever possible. Exploitation has been the rule from the beginning of time; the Egyptians, the Romans, the Babylonians, and all of the modern colonial

111

nations of the Western world are among the noteworthy proponents.

Yet political independence, which has always been a nation's due in the moral sense, is being accomplished today through world revolution. Since the end of World War II hundreds of millions of the world's people have received political independence. Pope John applauds this, saying that nations, like individuals, have a right to independence. They have a right to develop their proper genius, free of undue control by other nations, in order to make their unique contribution to mankind. Colonialism can no longer be tolerated in a world where people are growing more conscious of their personal dignity and originality.

In these times of complex international relations, the various nations recognize that order cannot be established on power. The contemporary condition of chaos has become intolerable, and the insistent demands of the world's people is for order. But on what principle is this order to be built? The Pope proposes the moral order, in which the rights and duties of man are paramount, and which consists in the principles of subsidiarity, independence, free immigration, economic development, and an unhampered exchange of information among nations. All of these are basically human rights transposed to a higher and broader level. And as a man must bring his conscience to any exercise of public authority, since it is an intrinsic part of his being, so too must nations retain a moral posture in their relations with each other. The only alternatives are military power and economic influence; but as the Pope points out further on, power is indeed a precarious instrument for order and peace in this thermonuclear age; ultimately, it can only mean the destruction of civilization.

In the past, many theorists viewed international relations as a type of power structure which ceased to bind when any state wished and was able to defy it. According to this doctrine, the will of the state was governed by nothing except an arbitrary choice of selfish alternatives, and since the state had no limits except the power milieu in which it operated, its will could be exercised unconditionally. The Holy Father maintains that arbitrary behavior of this kind contradicts correct reason and moral law, as is immediately evident when the logic of the power theory is examined. Because an arbitrary act of the will can be either right or wrong and has no constant framework which is always valid, it does not derive from rational control, and acts not controlled by reason have no ethical validity. To accept the power theory as the foundation of international laws and relationships, then, is to accept irrationality. This theory denies the existence of the bond among men which, as the Holy Father underscored in Part I, is founded on their human rights.

On the other hand, the ancient maxim *pacta sunt servanda,* treaties must be observed, is plausible when it is understood within its proper limits; it cannot stand by itself but must be deduced from the more general principle of the infinite value of the human person endowed with reason and liberty. This maxim —one among the many governing international relations—belongs to a system of rational truths that cannot be accepted by those who hold that the will of the individual state is supreme in its relations with other countries. Machiavelli, for example, advises the prudent ruler not to keep faith when by so doing it would be against his interest. Given this rejection of natural law and the concomitant proposition that no authority is higher than the individual state, international relations are reduced to a matter of power politics in which the weak are preyed upon by the strong. The Holy Father states that this is directly opposed to the moral law. There is an authority over the individual states, and this authority exists because the universal common good, including universal peace, cannot be procured by any one state.

Fortunately, the theory of state supremacy has been successfully challenged throughout the world, not only pragmatically but also in various schools of law and political science. To discern this general disapproval of power politics, it is only necessary to recall, as the Holy Father himself does, the Universal Declaration of the Rights of Man, approved by the General Assembly of the United Nations. This document rightly asserts, "The recognition of the dignity inherent in all members of the human family and of their equal and inalienable rights constitutes the foundation of liberty, justice, and peace in the world" (Introduction). If, as the signs indicate, a universal juridical order is evolving despite obstacles which make progress slow and laborious, it is certainly owing to men's common longing for peace and their increasingly widespread belief that an enduring peace can be founded only on a law of reason, a law of justice and liberty, rooted firmly in the recognition of the rights of the human person. Conversely, if the doctrine of unlimited state sovereignty were to prevail, the world would be condemned to perpetual instability and virtual anarchy. Pope John writes approvingly of the strides which have been made in recent years toward the rule of natural law, and as he points out, modern technology and weaponry have made absolute national sovereignty an item that the world can no longer afford.

Having discussed the moral foundation which underlies proper relations between states, the Holy Father begins an examination of the rules which govern these relations. He first considers the conditions necessary for truth to prevail among nations, for without truth no reasonable ordering of international relations is possible.

In Truth: ¶86–¶90

The common sense of *Pacem in terris* is unerring. When men become powerful, educated, or rich, they tend to think themselves better than those who are less fortunate. To affect superiority for such reasons is a great temptation for individuals and nations alike. In the United States, the institution of slavery led many white men to consider themselves superior to Negroes. The Holy Father has already branded racism as doctrinal error. It is incorrect to say that one nation is better than another because it is larger, or stronger, or richer, or more cultured. This would make human dignity depend on accidents of nature. Just as a newborn baby has the same rights and dignity as an adult, so it is with individual nations.

From this passive point of view, all nations must respect the rights and dignity of others, but there is also a positive point of view demanded by moral law. An individual has received gifts from God for the enrichment of others, and he has a social responsibility to develop them; similarily, nations have received power and riches not simply for themselves but in order to help other nations develop their own resources.

As shown previously, objective and subjective culture enrich each other in reciprocal development. This same phenomenon exists on the international plane. The rights of usage, knowledge, art, and economics do not belong to any one nation; they belong to the whole family of man, which develops from them the richest objective culture possible. This universal development of objective culture makes a subjective culture available to all men which is richer than that of any individual nation. The major responsibility for this progress belongs to the more developed nations, and it is not something to be used for the sake of prestige and vanity. On the contrary, these nations are obliged to redouble their disinterested efforts to aid other nations.

If it is true, then, that all men are equal by virtue of their human dignity, it must also be true that there can be no such thing as a superior race, the usual claim made to justify extreme nationalism or racism. Each ethnic, cultural, and political community has its proper genius, which must be preserved. This is evident from the fact that the diversity of men and nations is the source of their enrichment.

It is not true that some human beings are by nature superior and others inferior. All men are equal in their natural dignity. Consequently, there are no political communities that are superior by nature and none that are inferior by nature. All political communities are of equal natural dignity, since they are bodies whose membership is made up of these same human beings [¶ 89].

The Holy Father constantly brings us back to the bedrock of any human society: the inalienable and inviolable rights of the human person. These support the structure of the moral law which governs individuals and nations alike.

It is a fact well established by past history that stronger nations tend to dominate weaker nations. The history of Western colonialism is not very pleasant to examine, and its injustices and degradations provide a great deal of material for Communist propaganda. The so-called Christian countries of the West moved into other countries and cultures with the belief that they were superior. These colonial peoples, mainly nonwhites, were considered culturally inferior, even though they had cultures which had suited their needs for hundreds and even thousands of years. Under the delusion that skins of white make everything right, Westerners began their exploitation of these peoples, a practice that was to continue for centuries.

An unfortunate development of colonialism was the association of Christianity and Western imperialism. The great work of the Christian missions and colonial expansion occurred simultaneously, and most of the native populations came to look upon Christianity as a by-product of their exploitation. Coupled with this was the fact that missionaries themselves took too little account of the innate character and the culture of the native peoples. By and large, the methods the missionaries used to convert natives amounted to a process of Europeanization. Consequently, when the Europeans had to leave colonial lands, Christianity was in a precarious position. This interconnection of Europeanization and Christianization is probably one of the main reasons that despite many years of missionary activity, the Far East remains largely non-Christian. The activities of men like Father Roberto de Nobile and Father Vincent Lebbe were notable exceptions to the rule; their method was to propagate Christianity within the framework of the cultural milieu of the population. Where it was used, it worked well. But efforts of this kind were either crushed by conservative members of the Church as in de Nobile's case, or came too late, as in Lebbe's case. The Second Vatican Council is attempting to remedy the total situation.

There was a built-in irony in the association of colonialism and Christianity. As the colonies were being exploited, the native populations were being imbued with the Christian ideals of the equality of men and their right to live in independence and dignity. Furthermore, in their effort to make their colonies produce more effectively and efficiently, overlord nations introduced the immensely fruitful technology of the West. Many of the subject peoples, seeing this technology in operation, began to understand that man is no longer condemned by nature to live in disease and poverty. With these two tools—the realization that they had the same rights and dignity as the Europeans, and the technological means to achieve their proper place among men— the native populations had both the ideas and materials for a full-scale revolution at hand. And in the past two or three decades these colonies have struck for independence with marked success.

In the early history of colonialism, domination was primarily accomplished by military conquest, but this means is obviously out of style in a world of increasing political self-determination. Today, oppression is mainly economic and industrial, and those countries that are well developed in these ways have a great advantage over those that are not. In *Faith and the World,* Canon Dondeyne described the problem unambiguously:

There is economic slavery, and this is more important. For, as Hegel so realistically described it . . . , poverty as such does not act as a revolutionary force in history, but rather the poverty that is experienced as slavery, that is, when the slave whose labor supports production and creates riches has almost no share in the wealth. Economic slavery can easily coincide with political autonomy. . . . Economic slavery is just as dangerous for world peace as political domination, and the yoke of this slavery still lies heavily on most of the underdeveloped countries, not because they are poor and do not own anything, but because foreign powers control and exploit their natural resources for their own advantage.[1]

[1]Canon Albert Dondeyne, *Faith and the World* (Pittsburgh, Pa., 1963), p. 203.

Economic and industrial domination is obviously the principal type of domination about which the Holy Father speaks.

By and large, however, Western colonialism is now a matter of history, and with hindsight it is easy enough to detect past errors and beat our breasts over them. But wallowing in the mud is not the best way to get clean, so a more positive point of view must be developed. Modern technology has put at man's disposal the possibility of alleviating suffering and privation in many of these areas of the world. An economic liberation is now possible, for most of the material needs of mankind can be satisfied. The non-Christian Aldous Huxley has reminded modern man that "poverty and suffering ennoble only when they are voluntary. By involuntary poverty and suffering, men are made worse."[2] The Holy Father maintains that there is a grave obligation for the developed countries of the world to take up their responsibilities and, inspired by a true love of all men, to aid the underdeveloped countries while there is still time. In the contemporary world, mankind is truly becoming a unity, and peoples of different races, cultures, and countries are truly neighbors. The Christian's response to this reality must be an expansion of his love beyond the home, the neighborhood, and the nation to all men; he must suffer with the suffering in all parts of the world.

This effort to assist the poorer countries of the world could hold the key to the survival of the West and the regeneration of Christian ideals in modern man. The critical question today is whether the underdeveloped countries will turn to the disinterested efforts of the democracies or be deceived and enslaved by the promises of totalitarian states. In pointing out the responsibilities of wealthier nations to poorer, the Holy Father emphasizes that

[2]Aldous Huxley, *Brave New World* (New York, 1946), p. 269.

aid must be given in a disinterested way, motivated by a love for the originality and complete independence of the people to whom it is given. The economic slavery of former days must be eliminated.

Nations giving aid, Pope John points out, must not forget "that peoples can be highly sensitive, and with good reason, in matters touching their dignity and honor" (¶ 89). Donor nations, and the United States in particular, are often shocked by the seeming ingratitude of recipients of aid, an attitude that manifests itself in disagreements in international policy and at times in open resentment. This is a typically human reaction, albeit perhaps an irrational one. St. Vincent de Paul, who certainly had some experience in aiding the poor, reminds us: "The poor are our masters, terribly sensitive and exacting masters . . . It is only for your love alone that the poor will forgive you the bread that you give them." The saint's message, like Pope John's, is that disinterested aid means precisely that the donor nation should not expect a return of any kind.

In international relations, then, the Holy Father teaches that truth requires the elimination of racism and that all states are equal in dignity. This dignity, like that of the person, arises from its rights; among these are the right to existence, to self-development, and to the means necessary for self-development, including aid from without. To curtail any of these rights by economic or political exploitation is unjust and cannot be tolerated.

Concluding his discussion of truth as the first norm regulating international relations, the Holy Father states the need for objectivity in international communications.

Truth further demands that the various media of social communications made available by modern progress, which enable the nations to know each other better, be used with serene objectivity. That need not, of course, rule out any legitimate emphasis on the positive aspects of their way of life. But methods of information which fall short of the truth, and by the same token impair the reputation of this people or that, must be discarded [¶ 90].

The Holy Father asserts that a nation has a right to be well informed about other nations. In our modern international community, this has become a necessity for the peace. One mark of a totalitarian state is the strictures and biases imposed on the communications it gives and receives. A totalitarian state distorts information in order to keep its people in ignorance about the benefits of a free political, economic, and cultural order. This falsification is particularly apparent in what is commonly called propaganda.

The problem of correct information is not restricted to totalitarian countries. Every nation is tempted to justify itself, to show itself at its best to other nations. This is not illegitimate, but there must be some objectivity in international news reporting. Little is known, for example, of the terrible exploitation of the Cuban people by the Batista regime which laid the foundation for the Communist take-over. There was no talk during the dictator's rule of an invasion of Cuba, of the terrible menace of the enemy, and so on. The United States tolerated the Batista government because of commercial interests, which to the Cuban people were as bad as Communism. This point is made not to justify a Communist take-over but to demonstrate that the public information services have a grave obligation to report international news in a proper perspective. Equally misleading is the distorted image spread abroad by cinema and television of the "American way of life," which features sex, sports, sadism, and in general a sordid

121

materialism. Other nations have a right to a true image of what makes America a great nation: the Constitution, the Bill of Rights, and the sacred position and dignity of the individual.

In Justice: ¶91–¶93

Justice is the second important norm regulating international relations. By listing the right of nations to their own proper existence and development, and by concluding that justice demands respect for these rights, the Holy Father indirectly gives his approval to the movement toward independence being made by most of the world's hitherto dependent peoples, especially in Africa, Asia, and Oceania.

In recent times, great problems have arisen with the drive toward decolonization and independence. Through the fault of the colonial powers, many of the previously dependent nations of the world are almost incapable of assuming the highly technical responsibilities of independence. In the former Belgian Congo, for instance, there was and continues to be a great lack of trained personnel to run industry and government. This unfortunate situation has existed in most of the countries that received independence after World War II. The Pope notes the resultant danger that these new nations may become pawns in the power struggle between East and West. Though the Pope does not give a specific solution to this serious problem, he does suggest a general solution in Part IV of the encyclical: the world political community could assume the responsibility of teaching and training the personnel needed in a particular country, a job to be done impartially and with no ulterior motives.

Continuing his discussion on justice, the Holy Father deflects his attention from international relations *per se* and considers the problem of large and distinct minority groups that exist within nations, a problem which has moral repercussions throughout the international community.

The Treatment of Minorities: ¶94–¶97

The existence of independent minority groups within a larger community has always posed some very delicate problems for the public authority. A nation is usually composed of peoples of the same ethnic, linguistic, and cultural background, but there are many exceptions to this rule in modern states. The most evident example of this phenomenon to Americans is the United States itself. There have been various attempts to retain national minority divisions within this country by immigrant groups, like the Germans and the Poles. The pros and cons of such attempts were hotly debated for many years, and the sensitivity of various groups is still rather high. In effect, the cultural richness of most national groups has not been destroyed but rather has been integrated into the American experience by way of the "melting pot." In *Protestant—Catholic—Jew,* Will Herberg, the eminent Jewish scholar, maintains that the "melting pot" experience has not been completed, and the result is that while Americans no longer identify themselves as national groups, they still do as religious groups. The Catholic community, however, has generally accepted American culture and has adapted itself accordingly, as the dynamism of the Church in America seems to bear out. Though the Holy Father does not seem to be addressing this part of his letter to Americans—historically, the Holy See has been pleased with the development of American Catholicism—there is no comfort in the encyclical for American champions of splinter groups.

The Holy Father is writing, rather, about the large ethnic and cultural groups which have existed for a long period of time within certain national political communities, among them Belgium with its French and Flemish divisions, Spain with its various Basque and Catalan communities, Canada with its English and French cultures, the various tribes to be found in almost any African state, European and North African groups in Algeria, and various Jewish communities in a number of countries. The nation as a whole is sometimes in a precarious position. Unity of language, for example, facilitates exchange and communication, but at the same time it tends to destroy the unique culture of a minority group. As a type of defense mechanism, the minority group in turn exaggerates and exalts its originality to the point where it is detrimental to national unity and harmony. Recent evidence of this has been seen in Canada, where various fanatical elements in Quebec Province have been resorting to bombings in their fight for an independent Quebec.

In order that both extremes be avoided, the principle of subsidiarity must govern the relationship between the state and its various minority groups. Any attempt to legislate for these minority groups must always be in the interest of the common good, and never may any effort be made to weaken or destroy them. The great danger here is that in attempting to defend themselves against prejudice, these groups become "closed" and even hostile to the community's social progress. The balance is a delicate one, but the principles are clear. Nazi Germany has amply demonstrated what the arbitrary force of a nation can do to minorities. This stern lesson must not be forgotten.

Active Solidarity: ¶98–¶100

The world is becoming a community, that is, the nations are fast developing political, cultural, and economic dependency on one another. The Holy Father sees in this interdependency progress and enrichment for the whole human race. Each country may exercise its right to economic goods, but only within the context of mankind's common good. In this age, which has seen the conquest of many of the adversities of nature, it is intolerable that some nations are underdeveloped, not only economically but socially and culturally as well. Only 17 percent of the world's population live in the North Atlantic Community (Western Europe, Canada, and the United States), but this group consumes approximately 75 percent of the world's wealth. The remaining 83 percent of the world's population must somehow survive on only 25 percent of the wealth. That the United States consumes about half of the world's wealth and yet only constitutes 6 percent of its population brings the disparity between the have and have-not nations into sharper focus. As Father Twomey has stated:

And as if this trafficking in black human flesh was not enough, the so-called Christian nations of the world embarked on centuries of imperialism in Latin America, Africa, the Middle East, and the Far East Again the roll call is familiar: England, France, Holland, Spain and Portugal. What crimes have been committed in the name of Western imperialism.[3]

Perhaps the notion of enlightened self-interest may be interjected here. In aiding other nations to develop economic stability and prosperity, the helping nation encourages the creation of more markets, which in the long run will benefit itelf. The need

[3]Father Louis J. Twomey, S.J., *Social Order,* XIII (1963), 2–3.

for markets has caused many nations to see the fallacy of putting up high tariff walls. Since modern life has become complex and diversified, no country can be sufficient to itself. If one country undersells another, it courts disaster for all. In the last ten years, many nations have practiced a new concept of trade and exchange. The best-known and most successful example of this has been the European Common Market, which has used mutual aid to achieve a more diversified, richer, and stronger economy. Other reciprocal trade agreements have been instituted by the United States, Canada, Great Britain, and Japan, among others. The Holy Father feels that this general movement represents a more just and equitable consideration among nations and a further curtailment of the cut-throat competition which was characteristic of the nineteenth and early twentieth centuries.

But the Pope does not stop at the level of economic goods. These are first in the order of execution because without them man cannot live in dignity. There are other goods, however, which are primary in the order of intention, that man needs to live a full human life. These are education, culture, art, and in general all the nonmaterial goods which elevate the spirit of man. The human race as a whole has more richness and diversity than does any one particular culture, and it is man's intrinsic right to share in this universal patrimony. UNESCO has already instituted many programs for the interchange of cultural and educational experiences. The increase in the number of exchange students is a mutual enrichment for their native land and the host country. The Peace Corps is making a tremendously important human contribution. The increasing number of international exhibits and fairs and such programs as the Olympic games all aid in spreading the nonmaterial wealth of mankind. No individual community has such rich cultural and educational institutions that it cannot learn a great deal from its involvement with all of mankind.

The Holy Father has no puritanical suspicion of this world's goods. To him, they offer men "the possibility of perfection without limits." God has given this world to men, and men must develop it and use it for their enjoyment and enrichment. The Holy Father is happy to see progress and cooperation among men, for through cooperation men can come to understand one another, and through understanding to love one another. The Holy Father is optimistic. And his optimism stems directly from his view of man, who is a free agent under God and who has the task of developing creation for the social and cultural fruits he may reap. Progress in recent times has been rapid, thanks to improvements in science and technology.

Scientific developments in the past two hundred years have outstripped the combined advances of mankind in this area in all previous history. These have affected man not only quantitatively (more of everything for his health, comfort, and welfare) but to an even larger degree qualitatively. With our more perfect technology, servile work ("slavery" to work, some theologians say) has been reduced, and by controlling nature, man has ceased to be a slave to nature's reverses. Augmented productivity permits modern civilization effectively to eliminate much of its enormous economic inequalities; there now exists the possibility to end, or at least markedly alleviate, privation in the underdeveloped countries of the world.

Moreover, through advances in the social sciences, the course of social events can today be better understood and regulated. For example, many of the discoveries concerning social well-being have led to moderate but effective forms of socialism—broad medical and life insurance programs, workmen's compensation and unemployment funds, improvements in tax programs, and numerous other social advantages. These institutions are indispensable factors in making the rewards of technology accessible to a majority of the community's citizens. As a result of these changes, men can truly cooperate to master nature and advance human goals.

More and more, however, men and nations must turn their thoughts from a narrow nationalism to a disinterested internationalism. *International responsibility* is no longer a high-sounding moral phrase; it is a definite reality already operative in certain realms, as through the United Nations and its subsidiary organizations like UNESCO and WHO. Technology has brought about an era of humanity that is inescapably universal; civilization is becoming more cosmopolitan.

Still, the inherent drawbacks of today's technology and science cannot be denied, and cause great concern among modern thinkers. Here it is only necessary to observe the central difficulties. First of all, technical progress does not automatically mean the perfection of man. Technology can be used for a great good or great evil, and unless men of good will influence it toward the good, there is little hope of a satisfactory application. Second, material progress easily leads to materialism. What was once done by prayer is now done by medicine, and while religion has been called the opium of the people, opium is now the religion of the people. The truly Christian thinker, versed in both religion and technology, can help to re-establish the proper balance between technological advances and the religious life. Finally, modern society has tended to make men strangers to each other and slaves

to a system. This is a problem afflicting recent society as a whole
—even the Church—and more thought must be given to it by
theologians and sociologists alike.

Obviously, then, the modern age has many serious difficulties
to surmount. But it should not be forgotten that it also has advantages undreamed of in past centuries. The Holy Father thus
applauds the progress man has made and encourages Catholics to
work to solve the great problems that confront the modern world.

The Balance Among Population, Land, and Capital: ¶101–¶102

The first of the great modern problems that Pope John considers is overpopulation. Though he deals with the subject at some
length in *Mater et Magistra,* here he returns to it and offers one
solution—free immigration. To effect this solution, the various
artificial barriers set up by nations have to be removed. The
United States, for example, can support a much greater population than it has, but its immigration laws are highly restrictive;
on the contrary, France, various Latin American countries, and
Canada have liberal immigration laws which help mitigate the
world's population problem. Yet, given the difficulties involved in
wholesale migrations, the Holy Father concludes that it is better
when possible to bring raw materials to an overpopulated country
for development. This solution has been working in Japan for a
long time.

On December 24, 1948, Pius XII introduced the idea of free
migration in a discussion of the vital space needed by the family.
He said the possibility of migration must exist to facilitate com-

munication among different countries, basing his reasoning on the principle that the goods of this earth are destined for the use of all peoples. However, Father W. B. Gibbons, S.J., in the *Proceedings of the World Population Conference,* 1953, said that migration cannot solve all population problems. It is impractical to move large numbers of people from countries like China and India. For free migration to be effective, moreover, the migrants must have a culture similar to that of the people with whom they are to live; otherwise, there will be dissension. The best solution for a more equitable distribution of goods is economic aid, which the Holy Father treats later in the encyclical.

These observations, however, do not negate the fact that migration can serve as at least a partial solution to this momentous contemporary problem. Some countries, however, not only refuse to liberalize their immigration laws but exclude certain ethnic groups entirely. This kind of elimination is embodied in the present United States quota system, under which only a pitiful handful of specified nationals may enter the country annually. The National Catholic Welfare Conference is presently working to eliminate such discriminatory legislation. This practice is more blatant in Australia, which follows a stringent policy of excluding Orientals. The Australian Catholic hierarchy has courageously attacked this intolerant attitude.

The reason migration must be free is simple: man belongs primarily to the world community by virtue of his human nature; therefore, he has the right to go anywhere in the world that can offer him better social, economic, or political opportunities. Within the context of the universal common good, every state must generously allow men who are not born citizens to exercise the right to dwell within its boundaries.

The Problem of Political Refugees: ¶103–¶108

For those who think that the Holy Father has gone "soft" on Communism, the section of the encyclical on the plight of refugees—another grave contemporary problem—will be revealing. There can be no doubt that these paragraphs refer to the totalitarian Communist states that have not respected the essential rights of the individual. The escapees at the Berlin wall, Cuban refugees, Hungarian freedom fighters, and Hong Kong immigrants all bear witness to the denial of human rights to the citizens of Communist-dominated countries. The Pope repeatedly says that human rights are sacred and inviolable and that one of the central functions of the state is to promote these rights. But in the Communist doctrine the exact opposite is true: the state alone has rights, and persons are in its service as it supposedly evolves toward a classless society. All must be sacrificed to this end. In such a conception, the human person is simply a means, a cog in the omnipotent machinery of the state. When the Communists praised this encyclical soon after its appearance, the Vatican had to remind them of the essential point so incompatible with Communist ideology: the primacy of the human person over the state.

In view of this denial of human rights by totalitarian states, the Holy Father encourages free nations to welcome political refugees and to give them full citizenship in "a sufficient sphere of freedom within which they can lead a life worthy of man" (¶ 104). UNESCO has done much to facilitate the placing of refugees. Such men as Father Dominic Pire, the Belgian Dominican, must certainly be commended for their work among political refugees and displaced persons. The United States has been slow to receive expatriates. The extraordinary act of Congress permit-

131

ting the entrance of 100,000 Hungarians was a step in the right direction. Presently there is another bill before Congress to permit a limited number of refugees from Hong Kong into the U.S.; but this number could be increased. Since a tremendous number of Chinese who come to Hong Kong are returned by the British because there is no more room on the few non-Communist land areas and islands, the U.S. has the moral obligation of opening its gates to these people. Nothing could be dearer to the heart of the Pope, and nothing could be more in conformity with the American tradition, so eloquently expressed on the base of the Statue of Liberty: "Give me your poor and oppressed . . . ."

Disarmament; In Liberty; and Signs of the Times: ¶109–¶120 and ¶126–¶129

The Holy Father turns his attention to the last specific problem in this part of the encyclical, the most critical issue of disarmament. The arms race is a threat to the very survival of man on earth. Modern technology and science have done much to alleviate suffering and generally improve man's life, but they have also given him the absolute power to exterminate himself.

The Holy Father faces this Frankenstein with an intense and moving appeal to all nations, especially to those who are in the possession of nuclear arms, to cease the arms race at once. Pope John evidently feels that time is running out, that if the tensions between East and West are not alleviated the result may be disaster, by intent or by accident.

The danger is very great. It is estimated that the stockpiles of American and Russian nuclear weapons have an explosive value amounting to thousands of megatons, more than enough to obliterate all life from the earth. Never before has the entire family of man held its own life and death in its hands: this is a stark reality which must not be forgotten during international negotiations. Even Khrushchev has acknowledged this terrible potential in his answers to the Chinese Communists, who wish to spread the Communist revolution by war. Four nations already possess nuclear weapons, and it is estimated that in the next five years ten or more nations will develop or receive them. A minor difference or a limited war can easily trigger total war, even if none of the belligerents wishes it.

Because of this danger, the Holy Father pleads for arms control while there is still time. This was also urged by Pius XII, who advocated the placing of all nuclear arms under an international authority which would have the power to inspect anywhere in the world. Referring specifically to the United Nations, Pius XII said that it "ought to have the right and power of forestalling all military interventions of one state into another, whatever be the pretext under which it is effected, and also the right and power of assuming, by means of a sufficient police force, the safeguarding of order in the state which is threatened."[4]

Pope John first laments the fact that an enormous amount of money, time, and intelligence is being squandered on the production of armaments. If the American budget for the military alone is considered, his point is immediately obvious. Something in the neighborhood of $50 billion a year is spent to support the military establishment. To put it in perspective, this sum would solve most of the economic problems of every underdeveloped country of the world. Americans are willing to spend $50 billion for a Damoclean security, but raise heaven and earth to reduce

[4]Address of Pius XII as trans. in *The Pope Speaks,* III (1957), 331.

the few billion provided for humane work. Is the American budget an index to American values?

As the Holy Father points out, the only thing which restrains Moscow and Washington is the balance of terror, the fear of massive retaliation. Last year, the secretary of defense assured the world that the United States would destroy all the cities of Russia only if the U.S. were attacked first. Yet can there be any assurance of this? And what assurance is there that any limit to the arms race will be developed? There is none, and so each side aims an even bigger gun at the head of the other, insisting that it must do so because the other is doing so. The psychological effect of this is devastating. The same is true of nuclear testing. Each side tests in order to perfect a "bigger punch in a smaller load," again blaming the other for the "need" to test; and the fear of total annihilation grows proportionately.

The crux of the disarmament problem is effective controls. Where are these controls to come from, and who is to administer them? Pope John does not give a direct answer, but it is implicit in Part IV of the encyclical. There he states that the world community must safeguard and promote the common good of the whole human family. Since the armaments question intimately touches the health, safety, and even survival of the human family, the control of weapons must be put into the hands of the United Nations. He is following Pius XII, who also spoke on this same question: "We desire to see the authority of the United Nations strengthened, especially for effecting the general disarmament which We have so much at heart. . . . This must be under the strict obligation of international law. Only the United Nations at present is in a position to exact observance."[5]

Pope John gives three reasons for disarmament which are ulti-

[5]*Ibid.,* p. 334.

mately based on a reason both sides will understand, regardless of ideology: mutual survival.

In the first place, it is an objective demanded by reason. There can be, or at least there should be, no doubt that relations between states, as between individuals, should be regulated not by the force of arms but by the light of reason, by the rule, that is, of truth, of justice, and of active and sincere cooperation.

Secondly, We say that it is an objective earnestly to be desired in itself. Is there anyone who does not ardently yearn to see war banished, to see peace preserved and daily more firmly established?

And finally, it is an objective which will be a fruitful source of many benefits, for its advantages will be felt everywhere, by individuals, by families, by nations, by the whole human family. The warning of Pius XII still rings in Our ears: Nothing is lost by peace; everything may be lost by war [¶ 114–¶ 116].

By itself, however, the motive of survival is not sufficient to assure an effective settlement of the arms question, which must come out of mutual trust. Is trust possible? The past certainly gives no assurance for the future. The Geneva conferences have been stalemated again and again over an effective means of control. The only hope for disarmament seems to be in strengthening the authority of the United Nations and the world opinion exercised within its doors.

Since the discord cannot be solved by further discord, there must be negotiations in "the highest and most authoritative assemblies" of men (¶ 118). Given the consequences of nuclear conflict, the Holy Father finds it "hardly possible to imagine that in the atomic era war could be used as an instrument of justice" (¶ 127). The question must be settled by negotiation, not by rockets. This last statement will provoke much discussion: would the Holy Father have ruled out the use of all nuclear arms, even in a defensive war?

Pius XII justified limited atomic, bacteriological, and chemical warfare under special circumstances, and his words have been a source of contention between the so-called moderates, who would agree with him that the use of nuclear weapons is moral in certain cases, and the nuclear moralists, who categorically deny any possibility for a moral use of nuclear weapons. The thought of Pius XII can be summed up in the following way. All wars of aggression fall under the moral proscription. This idea is a modification of the traditional doctrine of war. In his Christmas Message of 1956, Pius XII justified a defensive war by any state that has been unjustly attacked. This theory of "just war" has long been the basis of the Church's traditional position between the distorted poles of pacificism and bellicosity. Defensive warfare must "be imposed by an obvious and extremely grave injustice" and not for any minor infraction. There are other conditions. All other avenues, such as negotiation and arbitration, must first be exhausted; there must be a proportion between the injustice incurred and "the damages that would be let loose by the injustice"; and there must be a "solid probability of success." Perhaps the most important condition imposed is the limitation on the use of force:

Even then, every effort must be made and every means taken to avoid nuclear war with the aid of international covenants, or to set limits on its use precise enough so that its effects will be confined to the strict demands of defense. In any case, when the employment of this means entails such an extension of the evil that it entirely escapes from the control of man, its use ought to be rejected as immoral. Here it is no longer a question of defense against injustice and of the necessary safeguard of legitimate possessions, but of the annihilation, pure and simple, of all human life within the radius of action. This is not lawful on any title.

Thus, Pius XII was willing to permit the limited use of nuclear weapons. Can this position be reconciled with the words of his successor that "it is hardly possible to imagine that in the atomic era war could be used as an instrument of justice"? Specifically, did John XXIII ban nuclear warfare alone? Such an interpretation seems to be a misrepresentation of the Pope's thought. An analysis of the whole paragraph in which this statement is contained indicates that the Holy Father's argument is based on a *de facto* view of an existing situation and not on a *de jure* view of a theoretical possibility, as is Pius XII's. This interpretation is in accordance with the pastoral character of Pope John. In theory, the use of nuclear weapons could conceivably be moral in certain circumstances, but given the past history of warfare, it is probable that they would not be used morally.

Nearly ten years elapsed between the statements of Pius XII and John XXIII, and the danger of nuclear war has only increased. For evident reasons, nuclear war is not the way to settle the differences that arise among nations. All nations recognize this, and all wish to outlaw nuclear weapons and put them under effective international control. Pope John greatly feared total nuclear war, and with good cause; it was this fear that moved him to make his intense appeal to the consciences of men at the crucial time in history. If the appeal has fallen on deaf ears, the future of mankind is most uncertain.

Morally speaking, the problem of the 'just war" has come into focus with special urgency in the nuclear age. Many Catholic moralists consider the concept a thing of the past, since one of the essential conditions of a just war is that the good to be accomplished be superior to the damages incurred. Many persons question whether this is any longer possible. Pius XII's statement on the evil of uncontrolled destruction must give pause to all Christians who live in an age which hundred-megaton bombs are becoming commonplace. It is impossible to imagine what good could be seen in a thousand square miles of absolute destruction. This is a hard reality to look on, but it must be faced, and now. It is from this realistic vantage point that Pope John faced this agony of mankind. The Holy Father retained his hope for a nonviolent solution of the world's distressing problems to his death, but unless Christians and all men of good will work to realize this hope, man might well say with Dante, *"Lasciate ogni speranza voi ch'entrate."*

Again Pope John writes, no matter how any of these serious problems are solved, relations between states must always be conducted within the context of liberty.

One must also bear in mind that relations between states should be based on freedom, that is to say, that no country may unjustly oppress others or unduly meddle in their affairs. On the contrary, all should help to develop in others a sense of responsibility, a spirit of enterprise, and an earnest desire to be the first to promote their own advancement in every field [¶ 120].

The Holy Father's understanding of the dignity of nations manifests itself in a spirit of respect and good will.

In the next few paragraphs, Pope John returns to one of his recurring concerns: the obligation of the economically developed countries to aid underdeveloped countries.

Progress of Economically Underdeveloped Countries: ¶121–¶125

The motives that the Holy Father suggests for giving aid should appeal to all men of good will. Their membership in the human family should impel them to help their poorer brothers. To Christians, a further motive is assigned: they are called upon to aid others by virtue of the mystical union of all men in Christ, either in fact or as a destiny to which all men are called.

The Pope reiterates his plea to the richer countries to increase, not decrease, their aid. He obviously includes the United States in his praise for what has been done since the end of World War II. Some $98 billion has been given in aid during this period. Yet with his praise for a job well done, he implicitly urges the richer nations to continue this work. In the United States, there seems to be a growing resentment against foreign aid and a desire to stop it as quickly as possible. Its opponents argue that it does no good and that it ultimately weakens our country. This argument is in direct conflict with what the Holy Father stated in *Mater et Magistra:*

> Perhaps the most pressing question of our day concerns the relationship between economically advanced commonwealths and those that are in the process of development. The former enjoy the conveniences of life; the latter experience dire poverty. . . . The nations that enjoy a sufficiency and abundance of everything may not overlook the plight of the other nations whose citizens experience such domestic problems that they are not able to enjoy basic human rights. . . . We are all responsible for the fact that populations are undernourished. Therefore, it is necessary to arouse a sense of responsibility in individuals and generally, especially among those more blessed with the world's goods.[6]

Since this is a critical period in history, the Holy Father continues, these are times for greater effort and sacrifice: "It is hoped that in the future the richer countries will make greater and greater efforts to provide developing countries with aid designed to promote sciences, technology, and economic life."[7]

[6]John XXIII's encyclical letter *Mater et Magistra,* in *AAS,* LIII (1961), 409, ¶ 157–¶ 158.
[7]*Ibid.,* p. 411, ¶ 165.

This should not be asking too much of a country that is willing to spend over $50 billion for defense, $25 billion for gambling, $30 billion for vacations, $5 billion for liquor, and more than $1 billion for cosmetics; all this spending occurred within the context of a gross national income of over $550 billion in 1962. If the United States is unwilling to give for the development and strengthening of millions of destitute people, it reveals itself as a nation which has lost its vision. On a scale of dollars, vacations are six times more important than millions of starving men, women, and children, and liquor is at least as important. If the Catholic subscribes to sentiment against foreign aid, then he has lost all right to the name *Catholic,* which, simply interpreted, means "solicitous of all men."

Pope John urges that aid be given to the poor in a disinterested fashion. The recipients must not be used to forward the political motives of either the East or the West. To the Holy Father, as to all men of good will, underdeveloped countries are worthy of aid in their own right: their citizens are our brothers in creation and in the redemption and in their supernatural destiny.

Part IV

The Relationship of Men and of Political
Communities With the World Community

IN many respects, Part IV is the most momentous section of the encyclical. For the first time in papal history, a relatively complete statement on the moral obligation to form an effective world community has been embodied in the text of an encyclical. This part of the letter will cause great consternation among Catholics who have consistently opposed any surrender of national sovereignty. The Holy Father argues that what was always a truth—the solidarity of the human race—has now become a pragmatic reality. As a consequence, the moral order demands the formation of a world community which will promote the rights of man on a worldwide scale.

Part IV of the encyclical deals specifically with the world political community which is now evolving toward a more perfect formulation. The basis for the world community is the need to promote rights and dignity of the human person as expressed in the Universal Declaration of Human Rights of the United Nations and elsewhere. For many reasons, these rights can no longer be effectively promoted by the individual states. But while technology has made the world a true community, this community existed before the advent of modern technology:

The unity of the human family has always existed, because its members were human beings all equal by virtue of their natural dignity. Hence there will always exist the objective need to promote in sufficient measure the universal common good, that is, the common good of the entire human family [¶ 132].

Two conclusions follow from this observation. First, the justification for a world political community does not depend on the consent of individual nations to relinquish sovereignty but on the moral law, which demands that the common good of the whole human family be reconciled with and adjusted to the subordinate rights of individual states. Since the common good, in this age of advanced technology, cannot be guaranteed by individual states, no matter how good their will, a superior political community must promote and guarantee the rights of the human family. From this comes the second conclusion: all men, and particularly all Catholics, have a serious obligation in conscience to aid, foster, and participate in this world community.

Today the universal common good poses problems of worldwide dimensions which cannot be adequately tackled or solved except by the efforts of public authorities endowed with a wideness of powers, structure, and means of the same proportions, that is, of public authorities which are in a position to operate in an effective manner on a worldwide basis. The moral order itself, therefore, demands that such a form of public authority be established [¶ 137].

If this is a demand of the moral order, then Catholic isolationists and those who would say that what is good for the nation is good for the world are obviously in opposition to a moral demand. There is an authority over and beyond that of the individual political community, and it exists not by force from above but by right from below, that is, from the moral order.

A cursory examination of international relations literature shows that almost all of the writers on the subject are "policy-orientated"; that is, their ambition is to become members of government and to shape the world to their ideals. In the name of the "scientific truth" that they have discovered, they vie with one another in formulating moral judgments on which is the best form of society. Soviet theorists, no less infatuated by science,

derive a morality from dialectic materialism. By and large, Eastern and Western theorists alike have rejected the moral order
based on natural law because it seemed to them to be outside
the realm of political reality, which alone, they claim, must
dictate policies in international relations. And what is even more
astonishing, most identify their discoveries with obligations of
conscience, whose autonomy they respect no more than did their
predecessors, who are now accused of obscurantism. So far are
they from respecting the autonomy of conscience, they aim at a
total subjection of moral judgment to the findings of science.
The result of these modern errors on both sides of the Iron
Curtain has been a proliferation of polluted illusions which, like
the skepticism they are now provoking, constitute an inadequate
instrument for guiding the builders of the international city of
man. To state the problem directly, the present historic crisis lacks
an ethical principle that can guide international society through
the jungle of ideologies which threaten the destruction of man.
Is there is common principle that can be used as a starting point
for a construction of modern international relations and law?

To make national interest the sole rule of political action is
futile, not to say insane. Yet until international law is effective,
individual states have the responsibility of safeguarding man's
existence. Writing on one aspect of this problem, Paul Ramsey
observed:

Within nations, the moral control of the use of armed force has
attained legal definition, just as human rights are also legal rights in
civil society. Our multinational world is characterized only by the
absence of legal status for the guarantee of human rights, the
absence of juridical resolution of conflict, and the absence of legal
institutionalism of the moral distinction between the legitimate and
the illegitimate use of force. . . . There can be no hope that our multi-

national world can move toward international justice upon the premise that . . . there is no distinction to be made between the just use of armed force and the unjust resort to purposeless and wholly indiscriminate violence.[1]

Until an international juridical convention has brought weapons of mass destruction under control—and this will be a great advancement in positive law—enemies may come to a moral agreement to condemn the use of such weapons. And the existence of a minimum good common to all men requires a clear distinction between purposeless and indiscriminate violence and a limited use of force. The principles upon which nations must agree in order to preserve the peace and ensure man's continued existence can be found in natural law. But the difficulty experienced not only by atheists but even by Christians in rediscovering the notion of natural law demonstrates the vast amount of work to be done to make it intelligible to modern man. Yet the work must be done, for as Thomas Merton puts it:

Is there another choice today? The western tradition of liberalism has always hoped to attain a more equable world order by peaceful collaboration among nations. This is also the doctrine of the Church. Father Delp and Count von Moltke hoped to build a new Germany on Christian principles. Pope John XXIII in his encyclical *Mater et Magistra* clarified and exposed these principles. If there remains a choice confronting man today, it is the crucial one between global destruction or global order. Those who imagine that in the nuclear age it may be possible to clear the way for a new order with nuclear weapons are even more deluded than the people who followed Hitler, and their error will be a thousand times more tragic, above all if they commit it in the hope of defending their religion.[2]

[1] Paul Ramsey, "A Return to the Theme of Just War," *World View,* (August, 1962), p. 220.

[2] Thomas Merton, "Spirituality for the Age of Overkill," *Continuum,* I (1963), 11–12.

Interdependence Between Political Communities; Existing Public Authority Is Not Equal to Requirements of the Universal Common Good: ¶130–¶135

The first paragraph of Part IV contains two main reasons that a world political community is demanded by the moral order itself: human solidarity under natural law, and technology.

The human race is a family, and each human being as well as each nation has a responsibility both to the state and to the whole of the humanity. The world's goods and resources have been created for all men, and not for any particular nation. The patrimony of the human race is the sum total of all the wealth of the individual nations and of the individual persons in those nations.

Yet who is to promote this common good of the human family? Who will see to it that one nation does not oppress another economically or militarily? Who will assure that the basic human rights of the human person are everywhere safeguarded? In times past, this might have been accomplished by various international agreements. Yet most nations have tended to follow imperialistic aims; one wonders whether the Holy Father had his tongue in his cheek when he wrote: "In times past, one would be justified in feeling that the public authorities of the different political communities might be in a position to provide for the universal common good. . ." (¶ 133). The history of Western colonialism has been for the most part one of greed and exploitation. Be that as it may, the former method of procuring the universal common good—if it ever existed—can no longer be utilized; it must give way to a superior political community which will look to the common good both impartially and effectively. If either of these qualities is missing, there is no hope of accomplishing the peace.

A second factor which has made the world aware of the solidarity of the human family, the Pope explains, is the tremendous advances in technology. Vast distances are almost nothing, and economics are such that the price of balsam in Oceania will influence the cabinetmakers of Italy and the dollmakers of Japan. In principle, economic and social goods could be available to all men. Because of the tremendous strides in science and technology, men are no longer under the necessity of being condemned to lives of poverty and sickness. Ours is a time which has the possibility of reaching the height of true democracy. As the Holy Father points out in Parts I and II of the encyclical, the world is in a position to recognize the rights of all men and to help all men *exercise* these rights.

In the opening paragraph of this section, the Holy Father cites certain technological conditions which can be called *elements of fact*. These elements of fact—rapid communication and interdependent economy, science, and culture—all point in the direction of world unity.

The means of communication have reduced the world's immensity. Europe is now only five hours from the United States by jet; astronauts now circle the *whole* globe in eighty minutes. The possibilities for the future are unlimited. Radios, telephones, and communication relays in space make possible an almost instantaneous reporting of news in every part of the globe. These means of communication have made men urgently aware of international relations.

The world's economic life has become interdependent because of rapid communications and a more diversified demand for goods and raw materials. Countries must plan their economic life in relation to that of other countries. If one country is undersold on the international marked by another, the whole balance of international payments is affected. This situation is becoming more apparent to individual nations, who are entering into mutual trade and tariff arrangements like the European Common Market in an attempt to cope with this economic reality.

Science and technology have become international endeavors. Scientific knowledge and methods have no national boundaries. If a scientist fails to keep pace with what is happening in his field throughout the world, he rapidly falls far behind his colleagues. The same is true in all of the technical specialties. Countries watch and capitalize on technical and scientific progress in other countries. It is not surprising that any up-to-date research center library must subscribe to at least two thousand periodicals from all over the world.

Culture is also becoming worldwide. With the increase in rapid communications, the contemporary world is developing an objective culture undreamed of in history. While each country retains and develops its proper genius, it is enriched by absorbing various elements from other cultures.

These factors have created a new historical situation. Each period of history has had a particular mission which society was called upon to accomplish. As new facts arose, new tasks and responsibilities had to be accepted and realized. The elements just enumerated have brought about a new historical epoch, characterized by an increasing interdependence among men. Logically the historical situation of our age urgently demands a world political community.

A juridical, economic, and moral superstructure must be created to correspond to existing infrastructures in international

148

society that have arisen, as Marx and Engels observed, out of material conditions. These thinkers attempted to demonstrate that the infrastructures created a superstructure of juridical, economic, and moral values, that is, existing economic conditions created certain spiritual values. This is not true. For example, deposits of ore do not create wealth but are only a necessary condition for wealth. In the same way, the infrastructures of a society are a necessary condition for the establishment of certain juridical, economic, and moral values, but the infrastructures do not create these values.

Along with these new international situations, there also arise new dangers. The elements of fact may be a great benefit to man, but they may also be harmful if they are controlled by the wrong men. The Holy Father has already pointed out that the same technical know-how which has permitted man to conquer hunger, disease, and other natural adversities has permitted him to develop a weaponry which can bring about the total destruction of the human race.

He insists as a consequence that all material progress must be accompanied by a corresponding moral and spiritual progress. And because the welfare of all men is at stake, there is a moral demand for a world political community that can effectively safeguard the security of all mankind.

Pius XII made the same argument in his first encyclical, *Summi Pontificatus*. He condemned all types of racism and exaggerated nationalism, as well as the legal positivism which furnished a defense for individual nations unwilling to diminish their sovereignty by submitting to the jurisdiction of an international tribunal. Pius XII reiterated this teaching in an address to the International Congress of Penal Law on October 3, 1953, in which he vigorously called for an international penal code which could be administered by an impartial world court and which would reach into the individual sovereign states.

The world political community must have true juridical power to settle disputes by an impartial application of international law. An international juridical tribunal, the International Court of Justice, is presently in existence, but it is made ineffective by the refusal of member nations to surrender their "sovereignty" in international disputes. Unless the International Court of Justice can be given enforcement powers, the world political community will remain impotent. Pius XII often mentioned that the biggest obstacle to world federalism is national sovereignty. In an address on December 23, 1956, he said that "the exercise of their rights as members of this organ [the United Nations] should be denied to states which refuse even the admission of observers, thus showing that their concept of state sovereignty threatens the very foundation of the United Nations."[3]

States often claim exterior sovereignty, that is, the power to do all that is necessary to be recognized as a state by others; they also claim an interior sovereignty, including the power to enjoin their citizens in all cases whatsoever. It must be remembered, however, that both types of state sovereignty are relative, and are always limited and modified by natural law. Relations between nations today are still based on the unconditional affirmation of the sovereignty of each nation. The Holy Father unequivocally declares that this concept is not in conformity with the moral demands of the modern world:

. . . the public authorities of the individual nations . . . are no longer capable of facing the task of finding an adequate solution to the [international] problems mentioned above. And this is not because of a lack of good will. . . .

[3]*The Pope Speaks,* III (1957), 331.

It can be said, therefore, that at this historical moment the present system of organization and the way its principle of authority operates on a world basis no longer correspond to the objective requirements of the universal common good [¶134–¶ 135].

An important reason for mankind's failure to develop an effective organization and principle of authority to meet contemporary problems is its inability or unwillingness to formulate and implement clear concept of what constitutes justice on an international plane. A proper understanding of international justice implies a basic social philosophy which contains those ideals common to all men, not simply within national confines.

By explaining the demands of the moral order, the Holy Father provides a firm basis for this proper concept of justice, which, simply stated, is the solicitude for all men by all men. In a sense, Pope John is only reiterating the biblical notion of the solidarity of all men because they are one family whose origin is God. More particularly, he is continuing the long tradition of Vitoria, Aquinas, Suarez, and Grotius, a tradition set aside because of the exaggerated notion of nationalism which arose in the fifteenth and sixteenth centuries and which continued unabated through the disaster of World War II. Because of this hiatus in the tradition, the sense of international solidarity may be said to be in its infant stage in the modern era, but the Holy Father reaffirms its fundamental importance.

Relations Between the Common Good and Public Authority in Historical Context; and Public Authority, Instituted by Common Consent and Not Imposed by Force: ¶136–¶138

Perhaps in times past the character of the world was such that the individual state could assure the common good, at least within its own boundaries; but that character has changed, and what perhaps was once sufficient is no longer so. The family of man needs an operative world state. To paraphrase the Preamble of the United States Constitution, a world authority is necessary to form a more perfect union of men, to establish justice, to ensure world tranquillity, to provide for common survival, and to secure the blessings of liberty for men and their posterity. Such an authority and such a world are possible, and they must be sought.

The possibility for a society of humanity has imposed a new responsibility on individual civil societies. In the Middle Ages it was thought that a civil society was perfect, that it had all of the means necessary to accomplish its ends. Today, certainly, the individual civil society requires international society to complete its means, that is, to solve problems with which the state cannot cope. Understanding this need, Pius XII said that though the diversity that exists among nations should be promoted, individual nations must remember that they are part of a worldwide society.

In the past it was also thought that a civil society had only negative obligations to international society, in that it was not to obstruct the realization of this international society. Now it is understood more clearly that the state has positive obligations to the international order. The individual nation should contribute an increasingly larger part to the more perfect society as its objective culture progresses. The richer members of a world community should thus contribute more than will poorer members, and should in particular shoulder more of the responsibility for the solution of international problems that demand solution. A quick examination of three of these problems—the right of usage, health, and cultural growth—will demonstrate that much cooperation is needed if any solutions are to be achieved. And it is well to point out that these three problems constitute only a small part of the task.

Pius XII called attention to the right of usage in his radio message on the Feast of Pentecost in 1941. Stressing the fact that he was talking to the whole world and not only to Catholics, Pope Pius insisted on the equitable distribution of economic goods because the right of usage is a universal right. All men of all nations must work together to achieve an equitable distribution of goods, and rich nations must help the less fortunate countries. This principle of mutual help is not unknown to the rich nations; in fact, this principle has been often used to justify colonization: since the goods of the earth belong to all men, those areas may be colonized whose inhabitants are incapable of producing the goods the lands are able to yield. Colonial powers, however, have studiously ignored the fact that the riches of their own countries are for the good of all men.

Moreover, colonial powers have a direct responsibility to those countries they have colonized, for the latter's underdevelopment is often a direct result of colonization. Colonial governments often adopted a *laissez-faire* policy toward the exploits of the colonizers. The colonized received much less than a fair share of the wealth amassed, so that the country received small enrichment from its resources and meager compensation for its labors. Furthermore, colonizers generally came to cultivate but one product for export, e.g., rubber, coffee, sugar. Such single-product economies scarcely fit a nation for independence, especially since its material prosperity hinges so perilously on the vagaries of a single world market.

The problem of equitable distribution of goods will be solved only when all nations accept and are guided by the principle of the right of usage: that the goods of this earth belong to all men. It is not enough to supply underdeveloped countries with the goods they need: they must be helped to produce on their own the goods that they need and the other goods that they are capable of producing: this means an indigenous and diversified economy. To help colonies and former colonies in their development, careful study and consideration must be given to their traditions, folkways, codes of morality, and other aspects of the social structure. Too often in the past, complete communities have been dispirited or even destroyed by the indiscriminate introduction of Western technology. Such well-meaning but deadly aid must be avoided.

Another problem which demands the attention of more prosperous societies is an adequate health program for the world. A more equitable distribution of the world's goods would certainly be of help, since two-thirds of the world's population is ill fed, ill clothed, and ill housed. The medical aspect of the health problem must also be attended to. The great advances made in medicine and sanitation must be made available to less-developed countries. Though many diseases in these countries have been eliminated or greatly reduced, much remains to be done. Great numbers of human lives can be saved from misery and death by the simplest of sanitary and medical help, and to deny this little seems monstrously inhuman.

A third problem that needs resolution is the lack of sufficient culture among men. That over half of the world's population is illiterate dramatically points up this tragic lack. Because man does not live by bread alone, the food for his spirit, his intellect, and his imagination is as necessary as wheat and livestock. But before any truly elevating culture can come to a country, the educational environment for its utilization must be prepared. For this purpose, UNESCO has sent trained specialists to help many governments establish fundamental education programs for their people and to train the native population to become educators in turn. This attempt presupposes that governments recognize the right of the people to at least this fundamental education. In *Evangelii praecones* Pius XII emphasized the devotion with which Catholic missions are to approach the problem of education. Since many Catholic countries and countries where Catholic missions are working have a high rate of illiteracy, the problem of spreading fundamental education should and must be of special concern for Catholics.

These three unresolved problems emphasize what has been said before: at the present moment in history, the Church, universal by nature, has a great opportunity to work along with international groups like UNESCO, FAO, WHO, and the International Court of Justice. And since this is the hour of the laity on the international as well as the parish level, Catholics have unprecedented opportunities to work for the good of mankind. The underdeveloped countries look to laymen for economic, medical, and cultural aid, as well as for the solid moral principles and religious values of Christianity. Pope John mentions this demand on the Christian explicitly in the last part of the encyclical.

The organization of the world community, which is an essential condition of peace, requires at least that certain fundamental political principles be held in common. In the Holy Father's view, any human society must be built on this basic premise. On the one hand, the principle of subsidiarity must be maintained to ensure that each nation, culture, or ethnic group may develop its own genius for the good of all. On the other, within a federated world community the autonomy of each member must have some limit; a state, for example, cannot be permitted to recognize the institution of slavery.

One can conceive of peaceful relations among nations with vastly differing outlooks, but the relations would be contractual in nature; such nations could not be integral members of the organic solidarity which is the international community. Antagonistic political ideals would make it impossible, for example, to establish a criterion by which an international court of justice could measure its decisions. Furthermore, as long as the principles of power politics and violence are maintained, disarmament or even the limitation of armed forces could not be seriously considered. And faithfulness to promises could never be expected.

In essence, every political unit requires a certain degree of homogeneity in political ideas and fundamental principles, a homogeneity which most states incorporate in their constitutions. This same homogeneity is required in the future world community. But this does not mean that individual nations will be yoked into an artificial uniformity; on the contrary, each nation of this community should maintain its unique ethnic, religious, and other cultural characteristics. It is in the regulation of its political relations with other nations that the world community may demand total cooperation. The exterior sovereign authority of individual nations will be transferred to the world community, which derives its very existence form the moral order. The ideal has been set, and men, particularly Catholics, must work toward a realization of that ideal. Pope John states it this way:

A public authority having worldwide power and endowed with the proper means for the efficacious pursuit of its objective, which is the universal common good in concrete form, must be set up by common accord and not imposed by force. The reason is that such an authority must be in a position to operate effectively; yet at the same time its action must be inspired by sincere and real impartiality. In other words, it must be an action aimed at satisfying the objective requirements of the universal common good. The difficulty is that there would be reason to fear that a supranational or worldwide public authority, imposed by force by the more powerful political communities, might be or might become an instrument of one-sided interests; and even should this not happen, it would be difficult for it to avoid all suspicion of partiality in its actions, and this would take away from the efficaciousness of its activity. Even though there may be pronounced differences between political communities as regards the degree of their economic development and their military power, they are all very sensitive as regards their juridical equality and their moral dignity. For that reason, they are right in not easily yielding in obedience to an authority imposed by force, or to an authority in whose creation they had no part, or to which they themselves did not decide to submit by conscious and free choice [¶ 138].

The Universal Common Good and Personal Rights; and the Principle of Subsidiarity: ¶139–¶141

International political ideals should be implemented in a world law, and this means giving a concrete form to the immutable and universal natural law. If world law were based on natural law, its criteria would be the same as for the law of individual nations, and these criteria would serve to safeguard and promote human and civil rights. As the Holy Father states:

Like the common good of individual political communities, so too the universal common good cannot be determined except by having regard to the human person. Therefore, the public authority of the world community too must have as its fundamental objective the recognition, respect, safeguarding, and promotion of the rights of the human person [¶ 139].

In order for the world community to be efficacious, then, it must be *democratic,* and it must be organized in the form of a political democracy. A democratic political organization presupposes a recognition of the principle of subsidiarity. The reason for this has recurred time and time again in the encyclical: each nation, each ethnic group, each cultural division must be respected and encouraged; each national family is to rule its own internal affairs, and the higher authority cannot take over what the inferior community can do by itself. The principle of subsidiarity should not seem strange to Americans. A direct illustration of it is Article 10 of the United States Constitution: "The powers not delegated to the United States by the Constitution, nor prohibited by it to the states, are reserved to the states respectively, or to the people."

By and large, this principle has worked well in the history of the United States, and there seems to be no reason that it should not in international affairs. Since each member of the international organization has an original genius which belongs to it alone, it must have the necessary freedom to develop its proper genius within the context of the common good. The Holy Father states this directly:

Just as within each political community the relations between individuals, families, intermediate associations, and public authority are governed by the principle of subsidiarity, so too the relations between the public authority of each political community and the public authority of the world community must be regulated by the light of the same principle. This means that the public authority of the world community must tackle and solve problems of an economic, social, political, or cultural character which are posed by the universal common good. For because of the vastness, complexity, and urgency of those problems, the public authorities of the individual states are not in a position to tackle them with any hope of resolving them satisfactorily.

The public authority of the world community is not intended to limit the sphere of action of the public authority of the individual political community, much less to take its place. On the contrary, its purpose is to create on a world basis an environment in which the public authorities of each political community, its citizens, and its intermediate associations can carry out their tasks, fulfill their duties, and exercise their rights with greater security [¶ 140–¶ 141].

Because individual nations can no longer cope with the international situation, the establishment of a worldwide authority with effective powers to enforce the rights of man is demanded by the moral order. Pope John now specifies his thought further: this authority potentially exists in the form of the United Nations.

Modern Developments: ¶142–¶145

The passage on modern developments is a perfect illustration of Pope John's ability to keep a proper balance between pietistic generalities which mean nothing and rigid specifications. The Pope sees that conventional diplomacy and power structures between individual states are no longer sufficient to preserve the peace and survival of mankind. He points out the need for a supranational body which is not simply a debating team but which is armed with the authority to enforce peace. Thus, he suggests that the United Nations be given greater power.

The Pope means what he says. While recognizing the imperfections of that organization, he maintains that it is the best man has so far developed, and he encourages the United Nations in the objectives expressed in the Universal Declaration of the Rights of Man. He expressly tells Catholics and all men of good will not only to join this supranational organization but also to help implement its objectives.

In times past there was an unreal interpretation of papal encyclicals by those who did not care for the trend of papal thought, but who still, at least in some way, wanted to remain loyal to the Church. The Pope, they would say, is not speaking of the United Nations (in spite of the fact that Pius XII had favorably spoken of it many times!)—this United Nations which is nothing more than a grab-bag of atheists and totalitarians, a tool of international Communism—he is really speaking about a world community that will only be possible when God is universally recognized. But this kind of evasion is no longer possible: John XXIII explicitly and unequivocally names the United Nations as that world organization of which he is thinking.

Pius XII said much the same thing. Referring to the United Nations as the present embodiment of this world community, Pius XII said:

> The United Nations ought to have the right and power of forestalling all military interventions of one state into another, whatever be the pretext under which it is effected, and also the right and power of assuming, by means of a sufficient police force, the safeguarding of order in the state which is threatened. . . . We desire to see the authority of the United Nations strengthened, especially for effecting general disarmament . . . under the strict obligation of international law. Only the United Nations at present is in a position to exact such observance.[4]

While Pius XII spoke frequently and favorably about the United Nations and its objectives, however, Pope John's explicit reference to the United Nations as a positive embodiment of his

[4] *The Pope Speaks,* III (1957), 331.

ideal is the first such reference in an encyclical, the authoritative document of the ordinary magisterium. There is no need here to go into the teaching authority of such a document; it is sufficient to say that as far as Catholics are concerned, the support of the United Nations is now a matter of conscience. A decision or some constituent element of the United Nations may be disputed, but the basic ideals of the organization can no longer be disputed.

This moral injunction is especially important for American Catholics, since they seem to manifest a massive reluctance to endorse any form of internationalism which requires the smallest surrender of American sovereignty. The American Catholic community was never in full sympathy with this side of Pope John's thought, and it has even failed in general to become acquainted with his thought. This encyclical will serve as a clear and authoritative rebuke to the numerous Catholics who have not relinquished their false notions of exaggerated nationalism and who thus have failed to appreciate the mind of the Holy See on this highly important issue. This same reminder was made by Cardinal Montini (now Pope Paul VI). Writing in the name of Pius XII, to the French periodical *Semaine sociale* in October, 1953, he said, "How many Catholics continue to shut themselves within the narrow confines of a chauvinistic nationalism incompatible with the courageous efforts to start a world community demanded by recent Popes?" Pope John simply extends and strengthens the Catholic's obligation to support a world community. But in mentioning the United Nations specifically, he also states that its essential duty is the promotion and protection of the human and civil rights of all men:

It is Our earnest wish that the United Nations Organization, in its structure and in its means, may become ever more equal to the magnitude and nobility of its tasks. May the day soon come when every human being will find therein an effective safeguard for the rights which derive directly from his dignity as a person and which are therefore universal, inviolate, and inalienable rights [¶ 145].

Part V
Pastoral Exhortations

THIS last section of the encyclical *Pacem in terris* is called "Pastoral Exhortations" because it spells out to Catholics specific areas for action and cooperation in public life. Catholics are called to help achieve any objective good, whatever its origin—Catholic, non-Catholic, or pagan; what matters is that the good be done, no matter who has conceived it. This attitude is evident in the Holy Father's own use of examples. For instance, the moral obligation to form a world community, political in nature and strong enough to protect and promote the universal common good, appears in the work of St. Thomas Aquinas, Vasques, and Vitoria. Its practical implementation, which was not attempted until recent times, took the form of the League of Nations followed by the United Nations. These organizations were not founded by Catholics, but their work is morally good. The United Nations therefore deserves the cooperation of all men of good will and especially of Catholics, who are trained from childhood to look upon all men of whatever nation or color as creatures made in the image of God, as redeemed by Christ, and as called to a common eternal and supernatural destiny. To judge from the Church's teaching, there should be no other group so well prepared in breadth and depth for international understanding.

Yet Catholics have isolated themselves from the rapidly changing world. The dynamic force of Catholicism has become mummified in the midst of a de-Christianized community, whereas it should infuse spiritual values into a world journeying to eternity. To realize how great this deficiency has been, Catholics need only recall three great events that are at the origin of our time and that continue to determine its specific character.

The first of these events was the foundation laid for various branches of modern science by Galileo, and later by Darwin and Freud. The shameful treatment of Galileo and the hostility to the beginnings of positive science are too well known to need further comment. The notions of evolution and psychoanalysis were also suspect in their early history, and in general, Catholics were the last to accept the findings of these men. The second of these events was the dissolution of the old forms of government and the birth of democratic regimes. The idea of religious freedom is only now beginning to find general favor in Catholic circles; this simple fact obviates any need to delve further into the painful blindness of Catholics during the nineteenth century to demo-cratic rule and their tenacious adherence to the passing culture of the Middle Ages. And third, the atheist Karl Marx made the social breakthrough in the latter half of the last century. The inhuman treatment of people on a social plane did not seem to bother Catholics until 1891. Even when Leo XIII published his social encyclical, *Rerum novarum,* many Catholics refused to follow his teachings; even in 1961, some Catholics called Pope John's *Mater et Magistra* a "venture in triviality."

In each of these modern revolutions, Catholics have not only lagged behind but have carped when progress became inevitable. When considering those great upheavals, a Catholic must confess to his shame that the Catholic community reacted very slowly to them, that it showed hesitancy and fear, and that it had its eye riveted on the past and not directed to the future. This blindness on the part of many Catholics has caused great harm to Chris-tianity. Each era has its own sensitivity to values in every realm of human activity, including religion and ethics; when Christians close their minds to the values pursued by their contemporaries, a dialogue between Christianity and the world becomes impossible. The modern world's complaint against Catholicism follows these lines, and can be summarized briefly. The Christian is by nature conservative and reactionary. His faith makes him long for a heavenly fatherland and imposes a revealed and unchangeable ethic on him. Therefore, the Christian is not fit to fulfill his hole in history with full freedom and independence. A Christian is less free than others, is less well equipped to tackle the problems of modern life, and is, in a certain sense, one doomed to "come always too late." In answer to this complaint, says Pope John in Part V, the laity must involve itself in the secular world as trained and dedicated Christians who are animated by faith and love.

In the Holy Father's concern with the errors of the past, he displayed his generous capacity to distinguish error from the person erring and basic truth from its false philosophical framework. This attitude was indeed admirable; it revealed a man whose honesty was as deep as his knowledge and who did not hesitate to accept good wherever he found it. This viewpoint, of course, is not new in the history of the Church. For almost two thousand years, she has defended the validity of pure reason in knowing truth. From the second-century Clement of Alexandria to the great twentieth-century paleontologist Pierre Teilhard de Chardin, her thinkers have encouraged and upheld the idea that man's finite mind is the image of God's infinite mind. To St. Thomas Aquinas, man's ability to reason and to know is *participatio operis rationalis ipsius Dei,* a participation in the knowledge of God.

In a finite but definite way, man is able to understand the reality of which he is a part. To some, animal-man lives on a tiny clod of dirt spinning around an inferior star in a second-rate galaxy which is only one of a million other galaxies. And what is a man in this immense panorama? He is everything because of the one essential difference that separates him from the rest of creation: he understands and can continue to understand the laws and movements of this huge and intricate universe. No atom, no animal, no star, no other part of this universe with its billions of miles and its immeasurable amounts of energy can ever understand one iota of itself. But this "thinking weed" of man can do this. To St. Thomas, all of creation is some kind of participation in the very nature of God, but because of his reason and knowledge, man shares in this participation most perfectly. In keeping with this understanding of man, St. Thomas, along with all of Christian tradition before and after him, was confident that every truth is a participation in the very knowledge of God, whether it comes from Scripture, philosophy, or science.

Since the whole of creation is God's work, it would be blasphemous to believe that what God has put in His natural creation could in any way contradict what He has revealed directly to man. Those who have tried to use modern science as a weapon against Christianity are ultimately confused, but Catholics who have thrown suspicion and distrust on science and its technological advances are even more confused. The Church in its continuous tradition has always rejected both these positions. Since man is capable of grasping truth, he has nothing to fear from it, no matter what kind. As St. Clement once said: "For thy foot shall not stumble, if thou attribute to Providence all good, whether it belongs to the Greeks or to us [Christians]. For God is the source of all good things; of some primarily, as of the Old and New Testaments; of others by consequence, as of philosophy." All knowledge, then, no matter how small or from what source, gives man a greater understanding of God and His creation. In short, all knowledge is a good we must strive to attain.

Squarely in the Church tradition, the Holy Father urges Catholics to pursue the good wherever they may find it. A Catholic layman has a duty in every area of human activity, and he must not be dissuaded from it by the fact that many of those about him are in error, for the work they do may also be a good in the most authentic and objective way.

The Duty of Taking Part in Public Life; Scientific Competence, Technical Capacity, and Professional Experience; and Action, the Outcome of Scientific-Technical-Professional Skill and Spiritual Values: ¶146–¶150

In opening his exhortations, the Holy Father refers to the well-known appeals to the laity which have appeared in papal teachings during the past hundred years. The most important of these appeals have signaled the increasing prominence of the layman's position in the Church, and to clarify this position, theologians have analyzed the relationship between terrestrial realities and the supernatural kingdom. From this analysis have derived significant and necessary responsibilities for the layman. If the world has become more secularistic, it is largely because Christians have failed to penetrate all of human endeavor with their presence, their contributions, and their leadership. As observed earlier in this commentary, unless material and technological progress receives its end and direction from men of faith, it is bound to be oriented to an exclusive this-worldness. If a spiritual direction is not given by men of faith, and especially Catholic laymen, it cannot be given at all.

To say that Christ and with Him the Christian are not interested in what is happening in this modern world is to reduce Christianity to a private pietistic affair of no consequence to man. Such a view is far from St. Paul's vision of the cosmic redemption, a vision which has influenced the work of almost all recent theologians. Modern theologians have done great service to Catholic thought by working toward a real, though yet incomplete, theological synthesis of the technological and scientific aspects of our era. The central factor in their synthesis is the position which the layman must play in the orientation and consecration of modern society to Christ.

Theologians say that the layman has his proper function in the Church, and it is to make the divine life incarnate in the temporal domain. In fulfilling this work, he will reach his own spiritual goal. The man of faith must enter fully and unreservedly into all areas of the temporal world to bring out the image of God contained in them. In the true biblical sense, he is God's lieutenant in creation, extending creation according to the image of God given to him through faith. His proper mortification will be to purify his own intentions continuously, and to accept the fact that at times he will see no direct connection between his work and the Kingdom of Christ; as faith is demanded to accept God's mysteries because reason can never fully understand them, so too the layman must have faith that his work in the world ultimately relates to the Kingdom of Christ. The layman partakes of the work of the Church in its full and cosmic sense. St. Paul had this grand and total vision of the Church and Christ's triumph through it; it is this same vision which the Holy Father proposes to Catholics.

To implement this vision, however, the Catholic layman must not only work in the world, he must imbue his work with Christian principles and values. And to do this, he must be truly conscious of the Christian value of his work. John XXIII continues his pastoral exhortation in this vein.

The Reconciling of Faith and Action; Education of the Whole Man; and Constant Endeavor: ¶151–¶156

It is not sufficient for the lay Christian simply to be present in the modern world in order to win it for Christ; he must be well trained in the technical and mechanical sciences in order to understand and participate in the extension of creation. This idea led to the formation of the Papal Volunteers for Latin America.

But without the orientation of faith, technology is self-destructive in the long run. The contemporary world has attained a technical development unknown in the history of man, but also, because of the lack of a superior ethical reference, this same world has been brought to the verge of total annihilation by its own technology. All too often, men and women are giants in knowledge of their particular field but midgets in their religious faith. This uneven education is dangerous, for religion and ethics become, at best, something of another world with no reference to the realities here below.

To bring knowledge and faith into a proper relation, the Christian must see all things as Christ sees them. His proper vocation as a layman is to find Christ's image within things and to consecrate himself to bringing it out. By virtue of creation, all is

Christ's *by right;* the great dignity of the lay Christian will be to help make it His *in fact,* enabling Christ to reproduce His image by extending it in creation. To change socioeconomic structures so that many can live as men and not as slaves, to humanize penal and labor laws, to guarantee a climate of freedom and tolerance for human beings and respect for property under just laws, to help underdeveloped countries attain the material capacity to live in decency and freedom, to work for peace in international organizations, to do research for better health that men may live their lives comparatively free from mortal dangers, to bring out the aspirations of man in art and writing, to fight racial discrimination by legislation and personal example, to work for equitable international trade agreements and tariffs—these direct works of Christ are but a few in the active litany of work that incorporates every aspect of man's temporal experience.

A grandiose tableau indeed presents itself to the Catholic layman. And strange as it may seem, only he can do this work. Communism and other totalitarian ideologies lead man only to self-destruction because they view the temporal wrongly. Only the Catholic layman has at his disposal the Christlike vision which will lead the temporal to the glorification of God and the service of all mankind. The Christian layman's is an awesome responsibility, and one which can be shirked only at the terrible price of losing the modern world and modern man for Christ. Every other religion or quasi-religion is radically incapable of such an endeavor because the endeavor is incompatible with its internal structure—the Eastern religions because they deny either matter itself or its positive value; and materialism, Communism, and secularism because they reject the realm of spirit.

Must men of today despair, then? A negative answer to this

171

grave theological question can be given only if an *integral* Christian theological synthesis is achieved. The contemporary world longs for a substantial soul, an inner meaning to its human values and accomplishments. And because of the uncertainty of the world's meaning, there is a constant temptation to condemn or belittle human and temporal realities. All of the dualistic doctrines which consider matter the work of an evil principle have yielded to this temptation. The material universe, nevertheless, is willed by God. And this world that man sees and touches is re-created by Christ's incarnation.

The whole object of Christian education must be to give unity of intention to scientific and technological endeavors. The fundamental unity of Christian action originates in the fact that God and Christ have one intention and one will with regard to all of creation. The idea of Christ will be the driving force of every authentic Christian work in the world. Pauline theology states clearly that all things are created for and through Christ, Who is the efficient and final cause. Yet a clear distinction must be made between the natural and supernatural: while both are united in the intention of the Creator and in the view of Christianity, faith does not fuse all of creation into a unity in which the temporal and eternal cannot be discriminated.

The unity of intention will be promoted by the layman when he furthers the Kingdom of Christ by infusing Christian attitudes into the temporal domain; this infusion is possible because no human activity is ever devoid of either spiritual or material aspects. The Christian idea (or if Christians fail, the materialistic, pragmatic, or other idea) becomes incarnate in words and actions. All of man's spiritual projects develop in the measure that they become the heart of his temporal work; conversely, a material project is the outward expression of a spiritual intention.

God wills this unity of faith without the confusion of domains in all of men's dimensions. The mistake of ancient Israel and even of men in the later Middle Ages was to put all human achievements and activities at the direct service of the supernatural end. The Renaissance emancipated human activity from this exclusive service, with both a good and a bad result. The good result was that human activity achieved the dignity willed by the Creator. The bad result was that human activity and its intention were dissociated from faith, a state of affairs known today as secularism. Yet this activity must receive its basic unity in God's intentions, for only through faith can man safeguard the ultimate dignity of human endeavor. By refusing faith in the intention of the Creator, man's modern civilization can terminate in a nonspiritual rationalism which can lead to temporal and terrestrial messianism. This is what has happened in Marxism, and this is what is happening in Western culture. It has been said with some truth that Communism is the logic of Christian messianism turned terrestrial. The layman has the difficult and awesome task of keeping the supernatural and natural domains intact, while at the same time procuring for the temporal, in which he is professionally engaged, the radical unity given to him by his faith.

Laymen must therefore be concerned with promoting human welfare in various sectors of society, since the Gospel has little chance of success in an environment where human values are threatened. Animated with the intentions of Christ, they must engage in and transform the temporal activities of the world. For example, the movement to fill the leisure time produced by technology with the beauties of creation found in music, drama, cultural radio and television programs, movies, and books is certainly a humanizing influence which corresponds to the deep wishes of Christ. Technology itself, with all its drawbacks, has produced a tremendous humanizing influence which cannot be denied: men have been freed from the slavery of the earth, from the dangers of famine, from the destructive forces of nature. Technological advances have certainly been according to the intention of the Creator, and the layman must learn to see God in and through them. The layman's education must be pursued along these lines because of the inherent difficulty in making the discriminations he must make. And the Holy Father is aware of these difficulties.

We deem it opportune to point out how difficult it is to understand clearly the relation between the objective requirements of justice and concrete situations, namely, to perceive the degrees and forms in which doctrinal principles and directives ought to be applied to reality [¶ 154].

If Christian education fails to train laymen's ability to perceive, understand, and solve these problems, laymen by themselves may never come to grasp the proper relationship between the city of man and the City of God; without this ability, they will have a tendency to separate the dynamic strength of their faith from the concrete realities of their workaday lives, and the result will be an ineffectual Sunday pietism or a negative, know-nothing gnosticism.

There is little doubt that much social progress has occurred since World War II. Through the work of agencies like UNESCO, FAO, and WHO, the standard of living has risen in practically all countries, deadly diseases and infant mortality rates have been reduced, trade is increasing, and cultural exchanges are growing. In the United States, Negroes have been making headway all over the country in their struggle for equal rights. Social security benefits, various kinds of pensions, sickness and old age insurance, better working conditions, increased leisure time, and improved cultural facilities are giving this country a security and wealth never before enjoyed by any country on earth. But the Holy Father reminds all men of good will that this is not the time for self-congratulation: "Accordingly, since each day we must endeavor to see how social reality can be brought more into line with objective justice, Our sons should not think of ceasing from the effort or of resting by the wayside" (¶ 155).

As the Holy Father points out, there is much work to be done. Internationally, the average per capita income in underdeveloped countries is less than $150 a year, while that of the richer countries is over $1500 a year. Domestically, Negroes are still denied many rights. Negroes and other minorities are not simply the victims of a series of iniquitous laws. As Michael Harrington has put it:

The American economy, the American society, and the American unconscious are all racist. So if all laws were framed to provide equal opportunity, a majority of Negroes would not be able to take full advantage of the change. The vast, silent, and automatic system directed against colored men and women would continue to exist.[1]

There are many more areas where much remains to be done— medical care for the aged, social justice for migrant workers, rehabilitation of depressed areas, retraining school dropouts; in sum, work is needed everywhere in society that man's rights and dignity are challenged.

[1]Michael Harrington, *The Other America: Poverty in the United States* (New York, 1962), p. 124.

Relations Between Catholics and Non-Catholics in Social and Economic Affairs: ¶157–¶160

This section of Pope John's exhortation should give the death blow to the Catholic ghetto mentality which inclines away from endeavors that have not been originated or inspired by Catholics. As mentioned earlier, the United Nations and the groups promoting civil rights for the Negro were not specifically Catholic in their formation or inspiration; they originated in the humanitarian impulses of non-Catholics. The Holy Father states that this should make little difference to Catholics because they must promote the good wherever it is found. As a matter of fact, he argues, the presence of a Catholic in these groups will serve as a beacon, a source of information and guidance to those not of the faith. But the Catholic should not enter these diverse organizations for the direct purpose of converting their members; his direct purpose is simply to accomplish good in a common endeavor with men of good will.

At the same time, of course, the Catholic will be a witness to Catholic truth, and this has a value in itself. Going into the world of temporal realities in this way, laymen become a sign for the world of unbelieving men to wonder at and contemplate. Christ was above all the supreme Sign of God; and by contemplating the words and works of Christ, men have to come to some conclusions concerning His mission. In his Gospel, St. John calls the extraordinary works of Christ not miracles but *semeia,* signs, in order to accent the supernatural aspect of the works, not simply their extraordinary character. These signs revealed the presence and personal action of God in Christ. To John, the signs were dramatic: an attitude took shape within a person according to the way he reacted to the sign he encountered, for the sign created the option between death and life, faith or unbelief.

In a similar way, the Christian becomes the faithful witness or sign of Christ to an unbelieving world. Since Christ is no longer physically present, this sign must now be expressed through the lay Christian in his effort to bring the Kingdom of Heaven into all temporal domains. The sign of Christ is needed in the domain of art where the image of man, who is created in the image of God, is so frequently falsified. There is the sign of Christian holiness that an Adenauer, a De Gaulle, or a De Gasperi expresses in the field of politics. Christ's heroic sign is portrayed in those Catholic organizations which take part in the United Nations, strengthening it and reminding it of its special duties to man. Speaking to the new minister of El Salvador, Pius XII urged the smaller nations and Catholic organizations not "to renounce the use of the forum of the United Nations but to employ it to prod the conscience of the world."[2] Then, there is the sign of the truly Christian home or of a parish whose people love one another deeply. Even so common a thing as an expression of warmhearted friendliness by a lay Christian testifies as a sign of Christ's charity to the world. All these, it might be added, are definite acts of worship on the part of the confirmed lay Christian. This testimony, this witness of Christ's love for the world, is a continuous and dynamic function of the character of the sacrament of confirmation.

Cooperation between various religious and secular groups, which Pope John's encyclical encourages, is increasing. The World Council of Churches has a long history of magnificent

[2]Cited in "Pius XII and the UN," Msgr. Harry C. Koenig, *Catholic Mind,* 52 (1954), 143.

social ventures. It would be a strong impetus toward Christian unity if Catholics and Protestants could join their efforts in promoting peace and accord where such cooperation has not existed before. Even mission countries will welcome this encouragement from the Holy Father. In places where the majority of the population is non-Christian, a unified effort in all endeavors that pertain to the common good can produce important results. This kind of cooperation would be particularly significant in countries with Moslem, Hindu, or Buddhist majorities.

It should be remembered, however, that the Holy Father's exhortation is by no means a radical break with former Catholic thought. As early as 1949, in a statement to the bishops of the world, the Holy Office encouraged Catholics "to meet . . . to take counsel together concerning joint action in the defense of the fundamental principles of Christianity and the natural law," and expressed approval of those "occasions when they meet to deal with the rebuilding of the social order and similar questions."[3]

Many Catholics fear to take part in social endeavors because they feel these endeavors are based on false or incomplete philosophical principles. This fear is no doubt warranted, but the Christian must have the courage and strength to pursue the good despite these difficulties. Pope John discusses this delicate question of the relationship between doctrinal principles and social realities.

It must be borne in mind, furthermore, that neither can false philosophical teachings regarding the nature, origin, and destiny of the universe and of man be identified with historical movements that have economic, social, cultural, or political ends, not even when these movements have originated from those teachings and have drawn and still draw inspiration therefrom. For these teachings, once they are

[3]"Ecclesia Catholica," quoted in G. K. Bell, ed., *Documents on Christian Unity* (London, 1952), p. 25.

drawn up and defined, remain always the same, while the movements, working on historical situations in constant evolution, cannot but be influenced by these latter and cannot avoid, therefore, being subject to changes, even of a profound nature. Besides, who can deny that those movements, insofar as they conform to the dictates of right reason and are interpreters of the lawful aspirations of the human person, contain elements that are positive and deserving of approval?

It can happen, then, that a drawing nearer together or a meeting for the attainment of some practical end, which was formerly deemed inopportune or unproductive, might now or in the future be considered opportune and useful. But to decide whether this moment has arrived, and also to lay down the ways and degrees in which work in common might be possible for the achievement of economic, social, cultural, and political ends which are honorable and useful—these are the problems which can only be solved with the virtue of prudence, which is the guiding light of the virtues that regulate the moral life, both individual and social. Therefore, so far as Catholics are concerned, this decision rests primarily with those who live and work in the specific sectors of human society in which those problems arise, always, however, in accordance with the principles of the natural law, with the social teaching of the Church, and with the directives of ecclesiastical authority. For it must not be forgotten that the Church has the right and duty not only to safeguard the principles of ethics and religion but also to intervene authoritatively with her children in the temporal sphere when there is a question of judging about the application of those principles to concrete cases [¶ 159–¶ 160].

These two paragraphs of the encyclical will probably cause a great deal of discussion among Catholics. First of all, Pope John makes a distinction between the good that various movements have accomplished and the false philosophical notions on which these movements may have been built. This statement may allude to the efforts of the nineteenth-century political democracies to separate Church and state so as to achieve and assure political independence. In the calm atmosphere of 1963, John XXIII could

179

look back and beyond the turbulence of the French Revolution, the Risorgimento, and the various anticlerical republics which arose in most of the countries of Europe. Each of these movements was conceived in an atmosphere hostile to the Church. Nevertheless, they all contained the seeds of tremendous goods which continue to mature in the modern world; political independence, social welfare insurance, universal suffrage, and equity of women before the law are only some of the goods which have resulted from these movements and which the Holy Father cites and praises throughout the encyclical.

Actually, the Holy Father's words are more probably an allusion to the social revolution of the nineteenth century, especially the rise of Marxism with its concern for social justice. Without a doubt, Karl Marx is one of the greatest figures of the modern era, and it is rather easy to distinguish his basic genius from the false philosophical premises on which he laid his social system. Marx, of course, was not the first to see social problems; nor was he the first thinker to give work, for example, serious consideration, but he was the first to make a systematic study of work and to produce a complete philosophy of work within the framework of the Hegelian dialectic. His genius was to see the importance of work as a basic human value and drive, which, in a limited sense, is a definition of man: *Homo œconomicus*. His system, however, was intimately tied up with many erroneous social and metaphysical doctrines, and thus was flatly rejected by Christian thinkers. This rejection ultimately had the unfortunate result of reinforcing the negative attitude toward material things and novel opinions, an attitude that had been present in Christian thought since the Council of Trent (1545–1563). And until the appearance of Leo XIII's *Rerum novarum* in 1891 and Pius XI's

Quadragesimo anno in 1931, no serious attention was given to the Christian meaning of work in particular or to the social order in general. The result of this long silence was what Pius XI called the loss of the working man to the Church.

In a sense, the Marxist allegation in the nineteenth century that religion is the opium of the people was valid. By neglecting the city of man and the temporal order, Catholics have contributed to the growth of Communism. Separated from its applied social principles, Catholicism is an eviscerated Christianity; it is disincarnate, and insofar as this is true, it is an "opium of the people." By their silence and even opposition, Catholics and other Christians refused to recognize social evils, and the swing to a terrestrial messianism, which Communism was and is, was almost inevitable. Marx served to prod the Christian conscience to an awareness of the terrible plight of the nineteenth-century working man; he was a prophet in his own right, preaching social justice on a world scale many years before Catholics even recognized its widespread lack. He was at the source of a ferment in the social order which, when pruned of its false philosophy, would not only become acceptable to the Christian but would become the inspiration for contemporary ideals of social justice.

The existence of world Communism, however, leads to another agonizing problem for the Christian, referred to above: a certain coexistence with Communism. The word *coexistence* is anathema to many Americans, but its reality must be faced. The Holy Father suggests certain possibilities. A "certain coexistence" is not indifferentism, but an existence in which the Church can retain its essential rights and exercise its vital functions.

For some forty years, the stand of the Catholic Church has been to have no dealings with Communist regimes. This course of action was dictated by a sound policy of nonappeasement, and the heroic martyrdom of many Christians attests to the firmness with which they adhered to this policy. But is martyrdom the only solution to this problem? Christian people must continue to live, even under a totalitarian regime. Cardinal Mindszenty has long been imprisoned in the American Embassy, but his heroism does not negate the fact that Hungary has practically no Catholic leadership because many of its dioceses are without bishops. Does not the Church have to think of them as well? The problem is very grave, and can only be solved in the best interests of all by those directly concerned. If some measure of freedom can be guaranteed, the Church cannot be accused of abetting Communism if it chooses to live a limited, though imperfect, life in such circumstances. This is what is happening in Poland, and with some success.

The Holy Father's major hope is for a gradual mitigation of the problems he has exposed throughout the encyclical. He writes that there are all too few working to restore the relations of social life according to truth, justice, love, and freedom, but these few he encourages "to persevere in their work with ever greater zeal" (¶ 164). In *Civil Disobedience,* Henry David Thoreau also spoke about just men: "A minority is powerless while it conforms to the majority; it is not even a minority then; but it is irresistible when it clogs by its whole weight." Contemporary wars and slaveries are different from those which Thoreau addressed, but the contemporary just man, and particularly the Christian, cannot allow injustice to destroy human dignity, even if he must fight alone.

Little by Little; and an Immense Task: ¶161–¶165

The Holy Father proposes an enlightened gradualism because, like all of human life, progress in institutions is made very slowly. Under certain sociological circumstances, a particular group of people can be totally blind to the immorality of a practice or an institution.

The original ferment of social justice has taken on a consciousness never before realized. A hundred years from now, man will consider such practices as segregation and racial discrimination in the same way that we now consider slavery. In the meantime, however, there must be heroic men and women who will take up the challenge. Social justice does not come about by itself; action is needed, not just wishful thinking and social theorizing. A hundred years of waiting by the Negro has not brought him recognition of his rights, but the reasoned, orderly, and lawful actions undertaken by the NAACP, sit-ins, and others have brought about a change. Without violence, and within the context of order and law, Negroes are beginning to win a recognition of what they have always had: their essential human rights as persons and citizens. This action means suffering, but if gradual means continue to produce results, the Negro will not have to create a violent revolution to gain the full recognition of his rights.

Regarding the fight for Negro rights, however, an objection must be lodged against the misuse of appeals to the cardinal virtue of prudence. It is a species of hypocrisy to tell the Negro that it is more "prudent" for him to "soft-peddle" his quest for equal rights because "the time is not ripe." Some white leaders advise everyone not to speak openly about the problem because it will cause "racial tension." But for whom? That tension, that pressure will be on the white racist who, consciously or not, wishes to perpetuate this degradation of other human beings. The Negro has been waiting for over a hundred years, but racists have not yet learned about the intrinsic dignity of man. It is the latter, not the Negro, who has grafted this caste system onto a "democratic" society. How much longer must the Negro wait to be treated, not as a white, for this is irrelevant and insulting, but as an American citizen?

Prudence is the moral virtue which directs a man to select the most efficient moral agency to eradicate "with all deliberate speed," as the Supreme Court put it, the injustices caused by race hatred. This requires a positive approach, a specific plan, a definite method, steps which no man could call imprudent.

Today, a greater emphasis on the moral virtues of fortitude and courage, rather than prudence, is needed to press forward positive programs for racial equality. Great courage and endurance will be demanded of those who stand up to racial prejudice in industry, employment, suburbia, in schooling and in housing. But as Thoreau said in *Civil Disobedience,* "Under a government which imprisons any unjustly, the true place for a just man is also in prison." These words take on a new sharpness in the light of recent events.

Gradualism, unfortunately, is not practiced all over the world. In countries where almost all the land and wealth are in the hands of a few who refuse to submit to basic social reforms, the situation tends to end in revolution. This, of course, is the case throughout Latin America. Gradualism is the rule, states the Pope, but what are these people to do when the few rich refuse them even a minimum share of the wealth? Southeast Asia is in a similar predicament.

It is natural that those who experience misery and frustration as a constant thing will drift toward Communism as a "way out." But Communism is not a causative factor in this drift; in Latin America, for example, Communism is not a cause, it is an effect. The cause is, in fact, the economic slavery to which the rich few, who dominate the armies and the governments, have reduced the masses in Latin America. Unless this slavery is eliminated Communism will surely triumph in Latin America, no matter how many blockades the American government proclaims.

The *Clay Report* pointed out that the United States has given money and arms—Viet Nam with its economic and political corruption is a case in point—in a losing attempt to stabilize native governments in Southeast Asia and Latin America, which, in the name of anticommunism, are opposed to all important and necessary social changes. Too often in the past, the United States has placed weak countries in the dilemma where they must stand still with the United States supporting their selfish rulers, or start moving with the Communists. This dilemma cannot be resolved unless the central, persistent, and unswerving policy of the United States is to offer these unhappy countries a third option, which is economic and social improvement without the totalitarian discipline of communism. What will be the outcome of the current crisis in these countries: the evolution or revolution? Time is rapidly running out both for them and for us.

The Prince of Peace: ¶166–¶173

In the normal use of the word, peace is more or less understood as the absence of war, and all efforts to secure peace are understood as measures taken to avoid war. But today there is much confusion whenever the word is mentioned. In certain American

circles, the expression *peace movement* is thought to represent a
piece of criminal naïveté at best or a sinister movement spread
abroad by international communism at worst. In Communist
jargon, on the other hand, all Westerners are imperialistic war-
mongers whose talk of peace is only lies. Pope John rises
above the stingy vocabulary men have allotted to peace and pene-
trates into the reality that peace can be firmly established only if
the order laid down by God is dutifully observed. Having shown
throughout the encyclical how this peace is to be achieved, the
Holy Father concludes that the peace which men seek on earth
is a participation in the very same peace which will only exist
fully in the final Kingdom of God. "In order that human society
may reflect as faithfully as possible the Kingdom of God, help
from on high is necessary" (¶ 168). Thus, it is Christ who brings
us peace.

In the Holy Father's mind, peace is not merely the absence of
war, a negative concept; rather, it is a positive concept whose component parts are "an order founded on truth, built according to
justice, vivified and integrated by charity, and put into practice in
freedom" (¶ 167). For Pope John, peace is a thing attainable in
this world. A terrestrial peace is an imperfect but real participation in the unique peace which is God's. In this concept of peace,
the absence of war is a result and not the definition of peace.
Peace is not man reconciled with himself after the class struggle,
as the Marxists have it; it is not an optimistic self-evolution of
humanity, as the eighteenth and nineteenth centuries thought; it
is not a pseudo-Christian escape into a hazy indifferentism which
has no effect in the world of the twentieth century; it is not the
evasive illusion of the Buddhist or the Hindu. Each of these attitudes is inadequate because it either indulges in the error of

negativity or attempts to escape from the problems of modern man.

The Holy Father's concept of peace avoids these errors, and in many ways, it is similar to that of St. Augustine. It demands a "tranquillity of order" with the consequent obligations on the human and Christian conscience. It is an order of justice that is animated by a disinterested love of all men because of the freedom which belongs to each man as God has created him. Peace, therefore, has several dimensions, each of which must be cultivated if this order is to be accomplished.

Peace is theological; that is, it consists in a moral order. Man is God's creation, and unless he understands what this entails, he errs at the outset. Man is sacred, and all of creation is oriented toward him and he toward God. Pius XII stated this aspect of man clearly:

> While it is true that the ills from which mankind is suffering today arise partly from economic unbalance and from the struggle for a more equitable distribution of the goods which God has given to man as a means of subsistence and progress; it is none the less true that their root goes deeper and is of an internal order connected with religious beliefs and moral convictions.[4]

In its deepest sense, then, a true peace can only be built upon the moral foundation established by God.

But peace is also political since man, in his social relations, is directed by law and political order. In this sense, peace depends upon man's ability to imbue national and international structures with the dignity and worth of the human person. In this effort, all Christian minds must come into operation, for Christ does

[4]Pius XII's encyclical letter *Summi Pontificatus,* in AAS, XXXI (1939), 324.

want peace on earth, an overflow, as it were, of the internal peace that unites God and man. This political aspect of peace directly involves a Christian humanism, because to assure a true peace, Christians must work in the world with increased vigor and courage. It cannot be stressed too often that the layman's vocation in the temporal order can be—and for the true follower of Christ must be—redemptive. Only laymen who are properly oriented in the temporal order can bring to the world Christ's inspiration and the Holy Spirit's dominion. By the work of the layman, the whole of man's experience in creation can become human and Christian, without becoming properly supernatural. The basic meaning of Christian humanism is that the Christian reflect the intention of Christ in all his terrestrial activities. And the more a Christian lives this point of view the more clearly will he see how Christian his "profane" vocation is. This in no way denies the nonsupernatural character of the layman's earthly work, but it does recognize the supernatural character of the Christian himself, and the duty he has, as a member of the Mystical Body of Christ, to infuse the light of the Gospel into terrestrial realities. The world cannot be considered unimportant to Christ merely because it is not supernatural.

The exercise of all human work is a religious activity in the widest sense; since the totality of human life is directed to God, all work is a service of God. The lawmaker who attempts to make a more perfect form of justice and the priest who distributes holy communion to the sick are both performing Christian actions, even though they are not of the same order. For the Christian who grasps this idea, there can be no possible opposition between civilization and religion, between the love of man and the love of God, between world peace and the Prince of peace.

This concept of political peace that proceeds from and is built upon moral considerations is obviously not a Catholic monopoly. It can and should be promoted by "all men of good will," since a more just world order will be more conducive to peace than an unjust world order. As Pope John indicates throughout Part V of the encyclical, this view of peace allows innumerable opportunities for cooperation between Catholics and non-Catholics. A little thought will reveal that the common denominator among "all men of good will" is much broader than their differences would suggest. There is a conception of order and justice, however minimal, that is accepted by many men, and even this minimum is sufficient to unite men in the effort to work out the various elements of peace.

Every man can make a contribution and give enlightenment if trust and confidence are present: "Meetings and agreements, in the various sectors of daily life, between believers and those who either do not believe or believe insufficiently because they adhere to error can be occasions for discovering truth and paying homage to it" (¶ 158). In international bodies, for example, men of all faiths and of no faith cooperate to alleviate hunger, disease, and privation, and the work of these is a positive effort in the creation of peace.

The Holy Father's words in Part V are simple and clear. They are the words of a Father whose heart aches because of the danger and conflict facing mankind. But they are also words of hope and optimism because, as he says, he relies on the grace of Christ, the Prince of peace. Numbers of the proposals in this encyclical are for many humanly impossible to achieve. But Christians have no right to confine their efforts to what can be humanly achieved; they derive their strength from Him Who said, "What is impossible to men is possible to God." This, indeed, is the great mystery in Christianity: God's will is accomplished in spite of men, and yet He will no nothing unless men cooperate with His grace. This reason is simple. He alone can influence and move the hearts of men by His grace without forcing them. In the words of St. Augustine, who summed up this mystery so well: "When God crowns our works, in reality He crowns His own works."

Paragraph 164 gives us an autobiographical note on John XXIII: "Admittedly, those who are endeavoring to restore the relations of social life according to the criteria mentioned above are not many. . . ." We might add that the reason there are not many is that to put such dynamic and living ideals into practice runs counter to the conservative and unbending frame of mind so many Catholics have toward the social teachings of the Church. This is one of the greatest tragedies of modern Catholicism: the social teachings of the Church can revolutionize mankind without a bloody revolution, and yet there are so few Catholics willing to heed the voice of their Mother.

Conclusion

THROUGHOUT *Pacem in terris,* John XXIII's central idea is direct and clear: the freedom, dignity, rights, and responsibilities of each human person are the only valid foundation upon which any national or international organization can be built. Universal peace is primarily a question of law, and this law, properly understood, must embody in concrete and operative structures the inalienable rights possessed by every human being. These rights, of an ethical and philosophical nature, are incompatible with any form of government which denies the ascendancy of the human person over all external political authority. Without this foundation, this inner life, any attempt to erect the formal structures of society or of peace will be wasted effort.

These concepts concerning the human person and his dignity are not intricate or biased, and they should be acceptable to all men of good will. Since Pope John based his encyclical upon natural law, the ideas it contains should evoke no objections from persons who oppose the Church's dogma. And since the essence of natural law is respect for the individual human being, the Pope's concepts and proposals are compatible with democracy, that form of human existence which even the Communist regimes claim to live in. The central purpose of any democratic society is to guarantee the civil rights of its citizens, and civil rights are simply legislated human rights. The Declaration of Independence states this point unambiguously: "That to secure these rights, governments are instituted among men . . . ," and "these rights" are those "certain inalienable rights" with which all men "are endowed by their Creator." Government, then, exists only to protect and promote human rights, and this has been Pope John's constant teaching throughout *Pacem in terris*. Father Kenealy has written:

> According to this philosophy, government is not an end in itself, but a means to an end. The end of government is justice—not merely the establishment of order, for order itself is a means. But in a mature civil society, justice too is but a means, and its end is liberty. And liberty is that condition of civil life which is necessary to enable all members of society to cooperate in peace and prosperity, to achieve their perfection, to attain their happiness, and thereby to fulfill in human dignity their divine destiny. Thus, the end of government and of law is adequately defined as a just and ordered liberty.[1]

The dignity of man derives from his "universal, inviolable, and inalienable" rights; he has these rights because he has been endowed by God with intelligence and free will. To put it another way, because man has the freedom to choose his own destiny, he must have the means, the rights, to effect his choice. Therefore, the supreme test of any society or government, national or international, will be the degree to which it protects and promotes these rights, thus enabling the human person to achieve his destiny in the liberty and dignity of a true son of God.

Because these are rights of the human person, no man may shirk his responsibility to participate in protecting and promoting them by pretending or by being deluded that this duty belongs to the state or to some nebulous authority outside himself. The decision to accept this responsibility belongs to the individual, by himself and with others. Men may either continue to suspect and

[1]"Racism Desecrates Liberty, Perverts Justice and Love," *Social Order,* 13 (1963) pp. 6–7.

mistrust each other or they may prove their mutual love and respect in this common endeavor. The time of decision has come; it cannot be put off. In times past, men could perhaps live separately in their own individual ghettos, and, ostrichlike, refuse to notice the rest of mankind; in the thermonuclear twentieth century, this is no longer possible. Men must either work and love and strive together for peace, or they will die together in an inferno of accentuated hate and suspicion. "And therefore never send to know for whom the bell tolls; it tolls for thee."

Pacem in Terris

Encyclical Letter of
His Holiness, John XXIII
By Divine Providence Pope

To the Venerable Brothers,
the Patriarchs, Primates,
Archbishops, Bishops,
and Other Local Ordinaries
in Peace and Communion
with the Apostolic See,
to the Clergy and Faithful
of the Whole World, and
to All Men of Good Will:

On Establishing Universal Peace
in Truth, Justice, Charity, and Liberty

PoPE JoHN XXIII

Venerable Brothers and Beloved Children,
Health and Apostolic Benediction

Introduction

Order in the Universe

1. Peace on earth, which men of every era have so eagerly yearned for, can be firmly established only if the order laid down by God be dutifully observed.

2. The progress of learning and the inventions of technology clearly show that, both in living things and in the forces of nature, an astonishing order reigns, and they also bear witness to the greatness of man, who can understand that order and create suitable instruments to harness those forces of nature and use them to his benefit.

3. But the progress of science and the inventions of technology show above all the infinite greatness of God, Who created the universe and man himself. He created all things out of nothing, pouring into them the abundance of His wisdom and goodness, so that the holy psalmist praises God in these words: O Lord, our Lord, how glorious is Your name over all the earth.[1] Elsewhere he says: How manifold are Your works, O Lord! In wisdom You have wrought them all.[2] God also created man in His own image and likeness,[3] endowed him with intelligence and freedom, and made him lord of creation, as the same psalmist declares in the words: You have made him little less than the angels, and crowned him with glory and honor. You have given him rule over the works of Your hands, putting all things under his feet.[4]

[1]Ps 8:1.
[2]Ps 103:24.
[3]See Gn 1:26.
[4]Ps 8:6–7.

197

Order in Human Beings

4. How strongly does the turmoil of individual men and peoples contrast with the perfect order of the universe! It is as if the relationships which bind them together could be controlled only by force.

5. But the Creator of the world has imprinted in man's heart an order which his conscience reveals to him and enjoins him to obey: They show the work of the Law written in their hearts. Their conscience bears witness to them.[5] And how could it be otherwise? For whatever God has made shows forth His infinite wisdom, and it is manifested more clearly in the things which have greater perfection.[6]

6. But fickleness of opinion often produces this error: many think that the relationships between men and states can be governed by the same laws as the forces and irrational elements of the universe, whereas the laws governing them are of quite a different kind and are to be sought elsewhere, namely, in the nature of man, where the Father of all things wrote them.

7. By these laws men are most admirably taught, first of all how they should conduct their mutual dealings; then how the relationships between the citizens and the public authorities of each state should be regulated; then how states should deal with one another; and finally how on the one hand individual men and states and on the other hand the community of all peoples should act toward each other, the establishment of such a world community of peoples being urgently demanded today by the requirements of the universal common good.

[5]Rom 2:15.
[6]See Ps 18:8–11.

Part I
Order Between Men

Every Man Is a Person with Rights and Duties

8. In the first place, it is necessary to speak of the order which should exist between men.

9. Any human society, if it is to be well ordered and productive, must lay down as a foundation this principle: that every human being is a person; his nature is endowed with intelligence and free will. By virtue of this, he has rights and duties of his own, flowing directly and simultaneously from his very nautre, which are therefore universal, inviolable, and inalienable.[7]

10. If we look upon the dignity of the human person in the light of divinely revealed truth, we cannot help but esteem it far more highly; for men are redeemed by the blood of Jesus Christ, they are by grace the children and friends of God and heirs of eternal glory.

Rights

The Right to Life and a Worthy Manner of Living

11. Beginning Our discussion of the rights of man, We see that every man has the right to life, to bodily integrity, and to the means which are necessary and suitable for the proper development of life; these are primarily food, clothing, shelter, rest, medical care, and finally the necessary social services. Therefore, a human being also has the right to security in cases of sickness, inability to work, widowhood, old age, unemployment, or in any other case in which he is deprived of the means of subsistence through no fault of his own.[8]

[7]See Pius XII's radio broadcast on Christmas Eve, 1942, in *Acta Apostolicae Sedis* (hereafter abbreviated *AAS*), XXXV (1943), 9–24; and John XXIII's sermon, January 4, 1963, in *AAS*, LV (1963), 89–91.

[8]See Pius XI's encyclical letter *Divini redemptoris*, in *AAS*, XXIX (1937), 78; and Pius XII's radio broadcast on the Feast of Pentecost, June 1, 1941, in *AAS*, XXXIII (1941), 195–205.

Rights Pertaining to Moral and Cultural Values

12. By the natural law every human being has the right to respect for his person, to his good reputation; the right to freedom in searching for truth and in expressing and communicating his opinions, and in pursuit of art, within the limits laid down by the moral order and the common good; and he has the right to be informed truthfully about public events.

13. The natural law also gives man the right to share in the benefits of culture, and therefore the right to a basic education and to technical and professional training in keeping with the stage of educational development in the country to which he belongs. Every effort should be made to ensure that persons be enabled, on the basis of merit, to go on to higher studies, so that, as far as possible, they may occupy posts and take on responsibilities in human society in accordance with their natural gifts and the skills they have acquired.[9]

The Right To Worship God According to an Upright Conscience

14. Every human being has the right to honor God according to the dictates of an upright conscience, and therefore the right to worship God privately and publicly. For, as Lactantius so clearly taught: We were created for the purpose of showing to the God Who bore us the submission we owe Him, of recognizing Him alone, and of serving Him. We are obliged and bound by this duty to God; from this religion itself receives its name.[10] And on this point Our Predecessor of immortal memory, Leo XIII, declared: This genuine, this honorable freedom of the sons of God, which most nobly protects the dignity of the human person, is greater than any violence or injustice; it has always been sought by the Church, and always most dear to her. This was the freedom which the apostles claimed with intrepid constancy, which the apologists defended with their writings, and which the martyrs in such numbers consecrated with their blood.[11]

[9]See Pius XII's radio broadcast on Christmas Eve, 1942, *loc. cit.*

[10]In *Divinae institutiones,* bk. IV, chap. 28, 2, in *Patrologiae Latinae* (hereafter abbreviated *PL*), VI, 535.

[11]Encyclical letter *Libertas praestantissimum,* in *Acta Leonis* (hereafter abbreviated *AL*), XIII, VIII (1888), 237–238.

The Right to Choose Freely One's State of Life

15. Human beings have the right to choose freely the state of life which they prefer, and therefore the right to establish a family, with equal rights and duties for man and woman, and also the right to follow a vocation to the priesthood or the religious life.[12]

16. The family, grounded on marriage freely contracted, monogamous and indissoluble, should be regarded as the first and natural cell of human society. To it should be given every consideration of an economic, social, cultural, and moral nature which will strengthen its stability and facilitate the fulfillment of its specific mission.

17. Parents, however, have the prior right in the support and education of their children.[13]

Rights Pertaining to Economic Life

18. We turn now to the sphere of economic affairs. Human beings have the natural right to free initiative in the economic field, and the right to work.[14]

19. Indissolubly linked with those rights is the right to working conditions in which physical health is not endangered, morals are safeguarded, and young people's moral development is not impaired. Women have the right to working conditions in accordance with their requirements and their duties as wives and mothers.[15]

20. From the dignity of the human person, there also arises the right to carry on economic activities according to the degree of responsibility of which one is capable.[16] Furthermore—and this must be specially emphasized—there is the right to a proper wage, determined according to the criteria of justice, and sufficient, therefore, in

[12]See Pius XII's radio broadcast on Christmas Eve, 1942, *loc. cit.*

[13]See Pius XI's encyclical letter *Casti connubii*, in *AAS*, XXII (1930), 539–592; and Pius XII's radio broadcast on Christmas Eve, 1942, *loc. cit.*

[14]See Pius XII's radio broadcast on the Feast of Pentecost, June 1, 1941, in *op. cit.*, p. 201.

[15]See Leo XIII's encyclical letter *Rerum novarum*, in *AL*, XIII, XI (1891), 128–129.

[16]See John XXIII's encyclical letter *Mater et Magistra*, in *AAS*, LIII (1961), 422.

proportion to the available resources to provide for the worker and his family a manner of living in keeping with the dignity of the human person. In this regard, Our Predecessor Pius XII said: To the personal duty to work imposed by nature, there corresponds and follows the natural right of each individual to make of his work the means to provide for his own life and the lives of his children, so profoundly is the empire of nature ordained for the preservation of man.[17]

21. The right to private property, even of productive goods, also derives from the nature of man. This right, as We have elsewhere declared, is an effective aid in safeguarding the dignity of the human person and the free exercise of responsibility in all fields of endeavor. Finally, it strengthens the stability and tranquillity of family life, thus contributing to the peace and prosperity of the commonwealth.[18]

22. However, it is opportune to point out that there is a social duty essentially inherent in the right of private property.[19]

The Right of Meeting and Association

23. From the fact that human beings are by nature social, there arises the right of assembly and association. They have also the right to give the societies of which they are members the form they consider most suitable for the aim they have in view, and to act within such societies on their own initiative and on their own responsibility in order to achieve their desired objectives.[20]

24. Moreover, as We Ourselves especially warned in the encyclical *Mater et Magistra,* it is most necessary that a wide variety of societies or intermediate bodies be established, equal to the task of accomplishing what the individual cannot by himself efficiently achieve. These

[17]See Pius XII's radio broadcast on the Feast of Pentecost, June 1, 1941, *loc. cit.*

[18]Encyclical letter *Mater et Magistra,* in *op. cit.,* p. 428.

[19]See *ibid.,* p. 430.

[20]See Leo XIII's encyclical letter *Rerum novarum,* in *op. cit.,* pp. 134–142; Pius XI's encyclical letter *Quadragesimo anno,* in *AAS,* XXIII (1931), 199–200; and Pius XII's encyclical letter *Sertum laetitiae,* in *AAS,* XXXI (1939), 635–644.

societies or intermediate bodies are to be regarded as an indispensable means in safeguarding the dignity and liberty of the human person, without harm to his sense of responsibility.[21]

The Right to Emigrate and Immigrate

25. Every human being has the right to freedom of movement and of residence within the confines of his own country; and, when there are just reasons for it, the right to emigrate to other countries and take up residence there.[22] The fact that one is a citizen of a particular state does not detract in any way from his membership in the human family as a whole, nor from his citizenship in the world community.

Rights in the Political Order

26. The dignity of the human person involves the right to take an active part in public affairs and to contribute one's part to the common good of the citizens. For, as Our Predecessor of happy memory, Pius XII, pointed out: The human individual, far from being an object and, as it were, a merely passive element in the social order, is in fact, must be, and must continue to be its subject, its foundation, and its end.[23]

27. The human person is also entitled to a juridical protection of his rights, a protection that should be efficacious, impartial, and inspired by the true norms of justice. As Our Predecessor Pius XII teaches: That perpetual privilege proper to man, by which there is assigned to each a definite and particular sphere of rights, immune from all arbitrary attacks, is the logical consequence of the order of justice willed by God.[24]

[21]See John XXIII's encyclical letter *Mater et Magistra*, in *op. cit.,* p. 430.

[22]See Pius XII's radio broadcast on Christmas Eve, 1952, in *AAS*, XLV (1953), 33–46.

[23]See Pius XII's radio broadcast on Christmas Eve, 1944, in *AAS*, XXXVII (1945), 12.

[24]See Pius XII's radio broadcast on Christmas Eve, 1942, in *op. cit.,* p. 21.

Duties

Rights and Duties Necessarily Linked in the One Person

28. The natural rights with which We have been dealing are, however, inseparably connected, in the very person who is their subject, with just as many respective duties; and rights as well as duties find their source, their sustenance, and their inviolability in the natural law which grants or enjoins them.

29. For example, the right of every man to life is correlative with the duty to preserve it; his right to a decent manner of living with the duty of living it becomingly; and his right to investigate the truth freely with the duty of seeking it and of possessing it ever more completely and profoundly.

Reciprocity of Rights and Duties Between Persons

30. Once this is admitted, it is also clear that, in human society, to one man's right there corresponds a duty in all other persons: the duty, namely, of acknowledging and respecting the right in question. For every fundamental human right draws its indestructible moral force from the natural law, which in granting it imposes a corresponding obligation. Those, therefore, who claim their own rights, yet altogether forget or neglect to carry out their respective duties, are people who build with one hand and destroy with the other.

Mutual Collaboration

31. Since men are social by nature they are meant to live with others and to work for one another's welfare. A well-ordered human society requires that men recognize and observe their mutual rights and duties. It also demands that each contribute generously to the establishment of a civic order in which rights and duties are ever more sincerely and effectively acknowledged and fulfilled.

32. It is not enough, for example, to acknowledge and respect every man's right to the means of subsistence: one must also strive to obtain that he actually has enough in the way of food and nourishment.

33.   The society of men must not only be organized but must also provide them with abundant resources. This certainly requires that they observe and recognize their mutual rights and duties; it also requires that they collaborate together in the many enterprises that modern civilization either allows or encourages or demands.

An Attitude of Responsibility

34.   The dignity of the human person also requires that every man enjoy the right to act freely and responsibly. For this reason, therefore, in social relations man should exercise his rights, fulfill his obligations, and, in the countless forms of collaboration with others, act chiefly on his own responsibility and initiative. This is to be done in such a way that each one acts on his own decision, out of set purpose and from a consciousness of his obligation, without being moved by force or pressure brought to bear on him externally. For any human society that is established on relations of force must be regarded as inhuman, inasmuch as the personality of its members is repressed or restricted, when in fact they should be provided with appropriate incentives and means for developing and perfecting themselves.

Social Life in Truth, Justice, Charity, and Freedom

35.   A political society is to be considered well ordered, beneficial, and in keeping with human dignity if it is grounded on truth. As the apostle Paul exhorts us: Wherefore, put away lying and speak truth each one with his neighbor, because we are members of one another.[25] This demands that reciprocal rights and duties be sincerely recognized. Furthermore, human society will be such as We have just described it if the citizens, guided by justice, apply themselves seriously to respecting the rights of others and discharging their own duties; if they are moved by such fervor of charity as to make their own the needs of others and share with others their own goods;

[25]Eph 4:25.

206

and if, finally, they work for a progressively closer fellowship in the world of spiritual values. Human society is realized in freedom, that is to say, in ways and means in keeping with the dignity of its citizens, who accept the responsibility of their actions precisely because they are by nature rational beings.

36. Human society, venerable brothers and beloved children, ought to be regarded above all as a spiritual reality in which men communicate knowledge to each other in the light of truth; in which they can enjoy their rights and fulfill their duties, and are inspired to strive for moral good. Society should enable men to share in and enjoy every legitimate expression of beauty, and encourage them constantly to pass on to others all that is best in themselves, while they strive to make their own the spiritual achievements of others. These are the spiritual values which continually give life and basic orientation to cultural expression, economic and social institutions, political movements and forms, laws, and all other structures by which society is outwardly established and constantly developed.

The Moral Order Has Its Objective Basis in God

37. The order which prevails in society is by nature moral. Grounded as it is in truth, it must function according to the norms of justice, it should be inspired and perfected by mutual love, and finally it should be brought to an ever more refined and human balance in freedom.

38. Now, an order of this kind, whose principles are universal, absolute, and unchangeable, has its ultimate source in the one true God, Who is personal and transcends human nature. Inasmuch as God is the first Truth and the highest Good, He alone is that deepest source from which human society can draw its vitality, if that society is to be well ordered, benefical and in keeping with human dignity.[26] As St. Thomas Aquinas says: Human reason is the norm of the human will, according to which its goodness is measured, because reason derives from the eternal law which is the divine reason itself. It is evident then that the goodness of the human will depends much more on the eternal law than on human reason.[27]

[26]See Pius XII's radio broadcast on Christmas Eve, 1942, in *op. cit.,* p. 14.
[27]*Summa Theologica* (hereafter abbreviated *ST*), I–II, q. 19, art. 4.

Characteristics of the Present Day

39. Our age has three distinctive characteristics

40. First of all, the working classes have gradually gained ground in economic and public affairs. They began by claiming their rights in the socioeconomic sphere; they extended their action then to claims on the political level; and finally they applied themselves to the acquisition of the benefits of a more refined culture. Today, therefore, workers all over the world refuse to be treated as if they were irrational objects without freedom, to be used at the arbitrary disposition of others. They insist that they be always regarded as men with a share in every sector of human society: in the social and economic sphere, in public life, and finally in the fields of learning and culture.

41. Secondly, it is obvious to everyone that women are now taking a part in public life. This is happening more rapidly perhaps in nations of Christian civilization and more slowly but widely among peoples who have inherited other traditions or cultures. Since women are becoming ever more conscious of their human dignity, they will not tolerate being treated as mere material instruments, but demand rights befitting a human person both in domestic and in public life.

42. Finally, the modern world, as compared with the recent past, has taken on an entirely new appearance in the field of social and political life. For since all nations have either achieved or are on the way to achieving independence, there will soon no longer exist a world divided into nations that rule others and nations that are subject to others.

43. Men all over the world have today—or will soon have—the rank of citizens in independent nations. No one wants to feel subject to political powers located outside his own country or ethnic group. For in our day, those attitudes are fading, despite their prevalence for so many hundreds of years, whereby some classes of men accepted an inferior position, while others demanded for themselves a superior position, on account of economic and social conditions, of sex, or of assigned rank within the political community.

44. On the contrary, the conviction that all men are equal by reason of their natural dignity has been generally accepted. Hence racial discrimination can in no way be justified, at least doctrinally or in theory. And this is of fundamental importance and significance

208

for the formation of human society according to those principles which We have outlined above. For if a man becomes conscious of his rights, he must become equally aware of his duties. Thus, he who possesses certain rights has likewise the duty to claim those rights as marks of his dignity, while all others have the obligation to acknowledge those rights and respect them.

45. When the relations of human society are expressed in terms of rights and duties, men become conscious of spiritual values, understand the meaning and significance of truth, justice, charity, and freedom, and become deeply aware that they belong to this world of values. Moreover, when moved by such concerns, they are brought to a better knowledge of the true God Who is personal and transcendent. Thus, they make the ties that bind them to God the solid foundations and supreme criterion of their lives, both of that life which they live interiorly in the depths of their own souls and of that in which they are united to other men in society.

Part II

Relations Between Individuals and the Public
Authorities Within a Single State

The Necessity and Divine Origin of Authority

46. Human society can be neither well ordered nor prosperous unless it has some people invested with legitimate authority to preserve its institutions and to devote themselves as far as is necessary to work and care for the good of all. These, however, derive their authority from God, as St. Paul teaches in the words, There exists no authority except from God.[28] These words of St. Paul are explained thus by St. John Chrysostom: What are you saying? Is every ruler appointed by God? I do not say that, he replies, for I am not dealing now with individual rulers, but with authority itself. What I say is, that it is the divine wisdom and not mere chance that has ordained that there should be government, that some should command and others obey.[29] Moreover, since God made men social by nature, and since no society can hold together unless some one be over all, directing all to strive earnestly for the common good, every civilized community must have a ruling authority, and this authority, no less than society itself, has its source in nature, and consequently has God for its author.[30]

47. But authority is not to be thought of as a force lacking all control. Indeed, since it has the power to command according to right reason, authority must derive its obligatory force from the moral order, which in turn has God for its first source and final end. Wherefore Our Predecessor of happy memory, Pius XII, said: That same absolute order of beings and their ends which presents man as an autonomous person, that is, as the subject of inviolable duties and rights, and as at once the basis of society and the purpose for which it exists, also includes the state as a necessary society invested with the authority without which it could not come into being or live. . . . And since this absolute order, as we learn from sound reason and especially from the Christian faith, can have no origin save in a

[28]Rom 13:1–6.

[29]*In Epistulam ad Romanos,* chap. 13, vv. 1–2, homil. XXIII; in *Patrologiae Graecae,* LX, 615.

[30]Leo XIII's encyclical letter *Immortale Dei,* in *AL,* XIII, V (1885), 120.

personal God Who is our Creator, it follows that the dignity of the state's authority is due to its sharing to some extent in the authority of God Himself.[31]

48. Hence, where authority uses as its only or its chief means either threats and fear of punishment or promises of rewards, it cannot effectively move men to promote the common good of all. Even if it did so move them, this would be altogether opposed to their dignity as men, endowed with reason and free will. As authority is chiefly concerned with moral force, it follows that civil authority must appeal primarily to the conscience of individual citizens, that is, to each one's duty to collaborate readily for the common good of all. Since by nature all men are equal in human dignity, it follows that no one may be coerced to perform interior acts. That is in the power of God alone, Who sees and judges the hidden designs of men's hearts.

49. Those, therefore, who have authority in the state may oblige men in conscience only if their authority is intrinsically related with the authority of God and shares in it.[32]

50. By this principle the dignity of the citizens is protected. When, in fact, men obey their rulers, it is not at all as men that they obey them, but through their obedience it is God, the provident Creator of all things, Whom they reverence, since He has decreed that men's dealings with one another should be regulated by an order which He Himself has established. Moreover, in showing this due reverence to God, men not only do not debase themselves but rather perfect and ennoble themselves. For to serve God is to rule.[33]

51. Since the right to command is required by the moral order and has its source in God, it follows that if civil authorities legislate for or allow anything that is contrary to that order and therefore contrary to the will of God, neither the laws made nor the authorizations granted can be binding on the consciences of the citizens, since we must obey God rather than men.[34] Otherwise, authority breaks down

[31]Pius XII's radio broadcast on Christmas Eve, 1944, in *op. cit.*, p. 15.

[32]See Leo XIII's encyclical letter *Diuturnum illud,* in *AL, XIII,* III (1881), 274.

[33]See *ibid.,* p. 278; and Leo XIII's encyclical letter *Immortale Dei,*

[34]Acts 5:29.

completely and results in shameful abuse. As St. Thomas Aquinas teaches: Human law has the true nature of law only insofar as it corresponds to right reason, and therefore is derived from the eternal law. Insofar as it falls short of right reason, a law is said to be a wicked law; and so, lacking the true nature of law, it is rather a kind of violence.[35]

52. It must not be concluded, however, because authority comes from God, that therefore men have no right to choose those who are to rule the state, to decide the form of government, and to determine both the way in which authority is to be exercised and its limits. It is thus clear that the doctrine which We have set forth is fully consonant with any truly democratic regime.[36]

Attainment of the Common Good Is the Purpose of the Public Authority

53. Inasmuch as individual men and intermediate groups are obliged to make their specific contributions to the common welfare, it especially follows that they should bring their own interests into harmony with the needs of the community. They should direct their goods and services toward goals which the civil authorities prescribe, in accord with the norms of justice, in due form, and within the limits of their competence. Manifestly, those who possess civil authority must make their prescriptions not only by acts properly accomplished but also by acts which clearly pertain to the welfare of the community or else can lead to the same.

54. Indeed, since the whole reason for the existence of civil authorities is the realization of the common good, it is clearly necessary that in pursuing this objective they should respect its essential elements, and at the same time conform their laws to the needs of a given historical situation.[37]

[35]*ST*, I–II, q. 93, art. 3, ad 2; see Pius XII's radio broadcast on Christmas Eve, 1944, in *op. cit.*, pp. 5–23.

[36]See Leo XIII's encyclical letter *Diuturnum illud*, in *op. cit.*, pp. 271–272; and Pius XII's radio broadcast on Christmas Eve, 1944, *loc. cit.*

[37]See Pius XII's radio broadcast on Christmas Eve, 1942, in *op. cit.*, p. 13; and Leo XIII's encyclical letter *Immortale Dei*, in *op. cit.*, p. 120.

Essentials of the Common Good

55. Assuredly, the ethnic characteristics of the various human groups are to be respected as constituent elements of the common good,[38] but these values and characteristics by no means exhaust the content of the common good. For the common good is intimately bound up with human nature. It can never exist fully and completely unless, its intimate nature and realization being what they are, the human person is taken into account.[39]

56. In the second place, the very nature of the common good requires that all members of the political community be entitled to share in it, although in different ways according to each one's tasks, merits, and circumstances. For this reason, every civil authority must take pains to promote the common good of all, without preference for any single citizen or civic group. As Our Predecessor of immortal memory, Leo XIII, has said: The civil power must not serve the advantage of any one individual, or of some few persons, inasmuch as it was established for the common good of all.[40] Considerations of justice and equity, however, can at times demand that those involved in civil government give more attention to the less fortunate members of the community, since they are less able to defend their rights and to assert their legitimate claims.[41]

57. In this context, We judge that attention should be called to the fact that the common good touches the whole man, the needs both of his body and of his soul. Hence it follows that the civil authorities must undertake to effect the common good by ways and means that are proper to them; that is, while respecting the hierarchy of values, they should promote simultaneously both the material and the spiritual welfare of the citizens.[42]

58. These principles are definitely implied in what was stated in Our encyclical *Mater et Magistra*, where We emphasized that the

[38]See Pius XII's encyclical letter *Summi Pontificatus*, in *AAS*, XXXI (1939), 412–453.

[39]See Pius XI's encyclical letter *Mit brennender Sorge*, in *AAS;* XXIX (1937), 159; and encyclical letter *Divini redemptoris*, in *op. cit.*, pp. 65–106.

[40]Encyclical letter *Immortale Dei*, in *op. cit.*, p. 121.

[41]See Leo XIII's encyclical letter *Rerum novarum*, in *op. cit.*, pp. 133–134.

[42]See Pius XII's encyclical letter *Summi Pontificatus*, in *op. cit.*, p. 433.

common good of all embraces the sum total of those conditions of social living whereby men are enabled to achieve their own integral perfection more fully and more easily.[43]

59. Men, however, composed as they are of bodies and immortal souls, can never in this mortal life succeed in satisfying all their needs or in attaining perfect happiness Therefore, all efforts made to promote the common good, far from endangering the eternal salvation of men, ought rather to serve to promote it.[44]

Responsibilities of the Public Authority, and Rights and Duties of Individuals

60. It is agreed that in our time the common good is chiefly guaranteed when personal rights and duties are maintained. The chief concern of civil authorities must therefore be to ensure that these rights are acknowledged, respected, coordinated with other rights, defended, and promoted, so that in this way each one may more easily carry out his duties. For to safeguard the inviolable rights of the human person, and to facilitate the fulfillment of his duties, should be the essential office of every public authority.[45]

61. This means that if any government does not acknowledge the rights of man or violates them, it not only fails in its duty, but its orders completely lack juridical force.[46]

Reconciliation and Protection of the Rights and Duties of Individuals

62. One of the fundamental duties of civil authorities, therefore, is to coordinate social relations in such fashion that the exercise of

[43]In *op. cit.*, p. 19.

[44]See Pius XI's encyclical letter *Quadragesimo anno,* in *op. cit.*, p. 215.

[45]See Pius XII's radio broadcast on the Feast of Pentecost, June 1, 1941, in *op. cit.*, p. 200.

[46]See Pius XI's encyclical letter *Mit brennender Sorge, loc. cit.*, and encyclical letter *Divini redemptoris,* in *op. cit.*, p. 79; and Pius XII's radio broadcast on Christmas Eve, 1942, in *op. cit.*, pp. 9–24.

one man's rights does not threaten others in the exercise of their own rights or hinder them in the fulfillment of their duties. Finally, the rights of all should be effectively safeguarded and, if they have been violated, completely restored.[47]

[47]See Pius XI's encyclical letter *Divini redemptoris,* in *op. cit.,* p. 81; and Pius XII's radio broadcast on Christmas Eve, 1942, *loc. cit.*

The Duty of Promoting the Rights of Individuals

63. It is also demanded by the common good that civil authorities should make earnest efforts to bring about a situation in which individual citizens can easily exercise their rights and fulfill their duties as well. For experience has taught us that unless these authorities take suitable action with regard to economic, political, and cultural matters, inequalities between the citizens tend to become more and more widespread, especially in the modern world, and as a result, a man's rights and duties in some way lack effectiveness.

64. It is therefore necessary that the administration give wholehearted and careful attention to the social as well as to the economic progress of the citizens, and to the development, in keeping with the development of the productive system, of such essential services as the building of roads, transportation, communications, water supply, housing, public health, facilitation of the practice of religion, and recreation facilities. It is necessary also that governments make efforts to see that insurance systems are made available to the citizens so that in case of misfortune or increased family responsibilities, no person will be without the necessary means to maintain a decent way of living. The government should make similarly effective efforts to see that those who are able to work can find employment in keeping with their aptitudes, and that each worker receives a wage in keeping with the laws of justice and equity. It should be equally the concern of civil authorities to ensure that workers be allowed their proper responsibility in the work undertaken in industrial organizaton, and to facilitate the establishment of intermediate groups which will make social life richer and more effective. Finally, it should be possible for all the citizens to share in their country's cultural advantages in an opportune manner and degree.

217

Harmonizing the Two Forms of Intervention by Public Authority

65. The common good requires that civil authorities maintain a careful balance between coordinating and protecting the rights of the citizens, on the one hand, and promoting them, on the other. It should not happen that certain individuals or social groups derive special advantage from the fact that their rights have received preferential protection. Nor should it happen that governments, in seeking to protect these rights, become obstacles to their full expression and free use. Nevertheless, it remains true that precautionary activities of public authorities in the economic field, although widespread and penetrating, should be such that they not only avoid restricting the freedom of private citizens but also increase it, so long as the basic rights of each individual person are preserved inviolate.[48]

66. The same principle should inspire the various steps which governments take in order to make it possible for the citizens more easily to exercise their rights and fulfill their duties in every sector of social life.

The Structure and Operation of the Public Authority

67. It is impossible to determine, once and for all, what is the most suitable form of government, or how civil authorities can most effectively fulfill their respective functions, that is, the legislative, judicial, and executive functions of the state.

68. In determining the structure and operation of government which a state is to have, great weight has to be given to the historical background and circumstances of the individual peoples, circumstances which will vary at different times and in different places. We consider, however, that it is in keeping with the innate demands of human nature that the state should take a form which embodies the threefold division of powers corresponding to the three principal functions of public authority. In that type of state, not only the official functions of government but also the mutual relations between citizens and public officials are set down according to law. This in itself affords protection to the citizens both in the enjoyment of their rights and in the fulfillment of their duties.

[48]See John XXIII's encyclical letter *Mater et Magistra*, in *op. cit.*, p. 415.

69. If, however, this juridical and political structure is to produce the advantages which may be expected of it, public officials must strive to meet the problems that arise in a way that conforms both to the complexities of the situation and to the proper exercise of their function. This requires that in constantly changing conditions legislators never forget the norms of morality, or constitutional provisions, or the objective requirements of the common good. Moreover, executive authorities must coordinate the activities of society with discretion, with a full knowledge of the law, and after a careful consideration of circumstances, and the courts must administer justice impartially and without being influenced by favoritism or pressure. The good order of society also demands that individual citizens and intermediate organizations should be effectively protected by law whenever they have rights to be exercised or obligations to be fulfilled. This protection should be granted to citizens both in their dealings with each other and in their relations with government agencies.[49]

Law and Conscience

70. It is unquestionable that a legal structure in conformity with the moral order and corresponding to the level of development of the political community is of great advantage to achievement of the common good.

71. And yet, social life in the modern world is so varied, complex, and dynamic that even a juridical structure which has been prudently and thoughtfully established is always inadequate for the needs of society.

72. It is also true that the relations of the citizens with each other, of citizens and intermediate groups with public authorities, and finally of the public authorities with one another are often so complex and so sensitive that they cannot be regulated by inflexible legal provisions. Such a situation therefore demands that the civil authorities have clear ideas about the nature and extent of their official duties if they wish to maintain the existing juridical structure in its basic

[49]See Pius XII's radio broadcast on Christmas Eve, 1942, in *op. cit.*, p. 21.

elements and principles, and at the same time meet the exigencies of social life, adapting their legislation to the changing social scene and solving new problems. They must be men of great equilibrium and integrity, competent and courageous enough to see at once what the situation requires and to take necessary action quickly and effectively.[50]

Citizens' Participation in Public Life

73. It is in keeping with their dignity as persons that human beings should take an active part in government, although the manner in which they share in it will depend on the level of development of the political community to which they belong.

74. Men will find new and extensive advantages in the fact that they are allowed to participate in government. In this situation, those who administer the government come into frequent contact with the citizens, and it is thus easier for them to learn what is really needed for the common good. The fact too that ministers of government hold office only for a limited time keeps them from growing stale and allows for their replacement in accordance with the demands of social progress.[51]

Characteristics of the Present Day

75. Accordingly, it follows that in our day, where there is question of organizing political communities juridically, it is required first of all that there be written in concise and limpid phraseology a charter of fundamental human rights, and that this be inserted in the basic law of the state.

76. Secondly, it is required that the constitution of each political community be formulated in proper legal terminology, and that there be defined therein the manner in which the state authorities are to be designated, how their mutual relations are to be regulated, what are

[50]See Pius XII's radio broadcast on Christmas Eve, 1944, in *op. cit.*, pp. 15–16.

[51]See Pius XII's radio broadcast on Christmas Eve, 1942, in *op. cit.*, p. 12.

to be their spheres of competence, and finally, the forms and systems they are obliged to follow in the performance of their office.

77. Finally, it is required that the relations between the government and the citizens be set forth in detail in terms of rights and duties, and that it be distinctly decreed that a major task of the government is that of recognizing, respecting, reconciling, protecting, and promoting the rights and duties of citizens.

78. It is of course impossible to accept the theory which professes to find the original and unique source of civic rights and duties, of the binding force of the constitution, and of a government's right to command in the mere will of human beings, individually or collectively.[52]

79. The desires to which We have referred, however, do clearly show that the men of our time have become increasingly conscious of their dignity as human persons. This awareness prompts them to claim a share in the public administration of their country, while it also accounts for the demand that their own inalienable and inviolable rights be protected by law. Nor is this sufficient; for men also demand that public officials be chosen in conformity with constitutional procedures, and that they perform their specific functions within the limits of law.

[52]Cf. Leo XIII's Apostolic Letter *Annum ingressi, Acta Leonis* XIII, XXII (1902–1903), pp. 52-80.

Part III
Relations Between States

80. Our Predecessors have constantly maintained, and We join them in reasserting, that political communities are reciprocally subjects to rights and duties. This means that their relationships also must be harmonized in truth, in justice, in a working solidarity, in liberty. For the same natural law which governs relations between individual human beings must also regulate the relations of political communities with one another.

81. This will be readily understood when one reflects that the individual representatives of political communities cannot put aside their personal dignity while they are acting in the name and interest of their countries, and that they cannot therefore violate the very law of nature by which they are bound, which is itself the moral law.

82. It would be absurd, moreover, even to imagine that men could surrender their own human attributes, or be compelled to do so, by the very fact of their appointment to public office. Rather, they have been given that noble assignment precisely because the wealth of their human endowments has earned them their reputation as outstanding members of the body politic.

83. Furthermore, authority to govern is a necessary requirement of the moral order in civil society. It may not be used against that order; and the very instant such an attempt was made, it would cease to bind. For the Lord Himself has warned: Hear, therefore, kings, and understand; learn, you magistrates of the earth's expense! Hearken, you who rule the multitude and lord it over throngs of peoples! Because authority was given you by the Lord and sovereignty by the Most High, Who shall probe your works and scrutinize your counsels![53]

84. Lastly, it is to be borne in mind that also in regulating the relations between political communities, authority is to be exercised for the achievement of the common good, which constitutes the reason for its existence.

85. But a fundamental factor of the common good is acknowledg-

[53]Wis 6:2–4.

224

ment of the moral order and respect for its prescriptions. Order between the political communities must be built upon the unshakable and unchangeable rock of the moral law, made manifest in the order of nature by the Creator Himself and by Him engraved on the hearts of men with letters that may never be effaced. . . . Like the rays of a gleaming beacon, its principles must guide the plans and policies of men and nations. These are the signals—of warning, safety, and smooth sailing—they will have to heed, if they would not see all their laborious efforts to establish a new order condemned to tempest and shipwreck.[54]

In Truth

86. First among the rules governing relations between political communities is that of truth. But truth requires the elimination of every trace of racism, and the consequent recognition of the principle that all states are by nature equal in dignity. Each of them accordingly is vested with the right to existence, to self-development, to the means necessary to its attainment, and to be the one primarily responsible for this self-development. Add to that the right of each to its good name and to the respect which is its due.

87. Very often, experience has taught us, individuals will be found to differ considerably in knowledge, virtue, talent, and wealth. Yet these inequalities must never be held to excuse any man's attempt to lord it over his neighbors unjustly. They constitute rather a source of greater responsibility in the contribution which each and every one must make toward mutual improvement.

88. Similarly, some nations may well have reached different levels of culture, civilization, or economic development. Neither is that a sufficient reason for some to take unjust advantage of their superiority over others; rather should they see in it an added motive for a more serious commitment to the common cause of social progress.

89. It is not true that some human beings are by nature superior and others inferior. All men are equal in their natural dignity. Consequently, there are no political communities that are superior by nature and none that are inferior by nature. All political communities

[54]See Pius XII's radio broadcast on Christmas Eve, 1941, in *AAS*, XXXIV (1942), 16.

are of equal natural dignity, since they are bodies whose membership is made up of these same human beings. Nor must it be forgotten, in this connection, that peoples can be highly sensitive, and with good reason, in matters touching their dignity and honor.

90. Truth further demands that the various media of social communications made available by modern progress, which enable the nations to know each other better, be used with serene objectivity. That need not, of course, rule out any legitimate emphasis on the positive aspects of their way of life. But methods of information which fall short of the truth, and by the same token impair the reputation of this people or that, must be discarded.[55]

In Justice

91. Moreover, relations between political communities are to be regulated by justice. This implies, in addition to recognition of their mutual rights, the fulfillment of their respective duties.

92. Political communities have the right to existence, to self-development, and to the means necessary for this. They have the right to play the leading part in the process of their own development and the right to their good name and due honors. From which it follows at one and the same time that they have also the corresponding duty of respecting these rights in others and of avoiding acts which violate them. Just as an individual man may not pursue his own interests to the detriment of other men, so, on the international level, one state may not develop itself by restricting or oppressing other states. St. Augustine rightly says, What are kingdoms without justice but bands of robbers?[56]

93. Not only can it happen, but it actually does happen that the advantages and conveniences which nations strive to acquire for themselves become objects of contention; nevertheless, the resulting disagreements must be settled, not by arms, nor by deceit or trickery, but rather in the only manner which is worthy of the dignity of man,

[55]See Pius XII's radio broadcast on Christmas Eve, 1940, in *AAS*, XXXIII (1941), 5–14.

[56]*De civitate Dei*, bk. IV, chap. 4, in *PL*, XLI, 115; see Pius XII's radio broadcast on Christmas Eve, 1939, in *AAS*, XXXII (1940), 5–13.

that is, by a mutual assessment of the reasons on both sides of the dispute, by a mature and objective investigation of the situation, and by an equitable reconciliation of differences of opinion.

The Treatment of Minorities

94. In this connection, especially noteworthy is the trend that since the nineteenth century has become quite prevalent and strong, namely, the desire of those of similar ancestry to be autonomous and to form a single nation. However, for various reasons, this has not always been possible, and hence minorities are found within the geographical limits of some other ethnic group, so that there have arisen problems of grave moment.

95. In the first place, it must be made clear that justice is seriously violated by whatever is done to limit the strength and numerical increase of these lesser peoples; the injustice is even more serious if such sinful projects are aimed at the very extinction of these groups.

96. On the other hand, the demands of justice are admirably observed by those civil authorities who promote the human welfare of those citizens belonging to a smaller ethnic group, particularly as regards their language, the development of their natural gifts, their ancestral customs, and their accomplishments and endeavors in the economic order.[57]

97. It should be noted, however, that these minority groups, either because of a reaction to their present situation or because of their historical difficulties, are often inclined to exalt beyond due measure anything proper to their own people, so as to place them even above human values, as if what is good for humanity were to be at the service of what is good for the ethnic groups themselves. Reason rather demands that these very people recognize also the advantages that accrue to them from their peculiar circumstances; for instance, no small contribution is made toward the development of their particular talents and spirit by their daily dealings with people who have grown up in a different culture. This, however,

[57]See Pius XII's radio broadcast on Christmas Eve, 1941, in *op. cit.,* pp. 10–21.

will be true only if the minorities, in their relations with the peoples around them, show an interest in the customs and institutions of these same peoples. It will not be true if they sow discord, which can cause considerable damage and choke off the development of nations.

Active Solidarity

98. Because relations between states must be regulated by the norms of truth and justice, they should also derive great benefits from active solidarity, through mutual cooperation on various levels, such as, in our own times, has already taken place with laudable results in the economic, social, political, educational, health, and sport spheres. We must remember that of its very nature civil authority exists not to confine its people within the boundaries of their nation but rather to protect, above all else, the common good of that particular civil society, which certainly cannot be divorced from the common good of the entire human family.

99. This entails not only that civil societies should pursue their particular interests without hurting others but also that they should join forces and plans whenever the efforts of an individual government cannot achieve its desired goals; but in the execution of such common efforts, great care must be taken lest what helps some nations should injure others.

100. Furthermore, the universal common good requires that in every nation friendly relations be fostered in all fields between the citizen and their intermediate societies. There are groupings of people of more or less different ethnic backgrounds. However, the elements which characterize an ethnic group must not be transformed into a watertight compartment in which human beings are prevented from communicating with their fellow men belonging to different ethnic groups. That would contrast with our contemporary situation, in which the distances separating peoples have been almost wiped out. Nor can one overlook the fact that even though human beings differ from one another by virtue of their ethnic peculiarities, they all possess certain essential common elements of considerable importance whereby they can progressively develop and perfect themselves,

228

especially in the realm of spiritual values. They have the right and duty, therefore, to live in communion with one another.

The Balance Among Population, Land, and Capital

101. As everybody knows, there are countries with an abundance of arable land and a scarcity of manpower, while in other countries there is no proportion between natural resources and the capital available. This demands that peoples should set up relationships of mutual collaboration, facilitating the circulation from one to the other of goods, capital, and manpower.[58]

102. Here We deem it opportune to remark that whenever possible the work to be done should be taken to the workers, not vice versa. In this way a possibility of a better future is offered to many persons without their being forced to leave their own environment in order to seek residence elsewhere, which almost always entails the heartache of separation and difficult periods of adjustment and social integration.

The Problem of Political Refugees

103. The sentiment of universal fatherhood which the Lord has placed in Our heart makes Us feel profound sadness in considering the phenomenon of political refugees: a phenomenon which has assumed large proportions and which always hides numberless and acute sufferings.

104. Such expatriations show that there are some political regimes which do not guarantee for individual citizens a sufficient sphere of freedom within which they can lead a life worthy of man. In fact, under those regimes even the very right to freedom is either called into question or openly denied. This undoubtedly is a radical inversion of the order of human society, because the reason for the existence of public authority is to promote the common good, a fundamental element of which is to recognize freedom and to safeguard it.

[58]See John XXIII's encyclical letter *Mater et Magistra,* in *op. cit.,* p. 439.

105. At this point it is not out of place to recall that exiles are persons, and that all their rights as persons must be recognized. Refugees do not lose these rights simply because they have been deprived of citizenship in their national state.

106. Now, among the rights of a human person there must be included that by which a man may enter a political community where he hopes he can more fittingly provide a future for himself and his dependents. Wherefore, as far as the common good rightly understood permits, it is the duty of that state to accept immigrants seeking to become members of a new society.

107. Wherefore, on this occasion, We publicly approve and commend every undertaking, founded on the principles of human solidarity and Christian charity, which aims at making migration of persons from one country to another less painful.

108. And We will be permitted to signal for the attention and gratitude of all right-minded persons the manifold work which specialized international agencies are carrying out in this very delicate field.

Disarmament

109. On the other hand, it is with deep sorrow that We note the enormous stocks of armament that have been and still are being made in more economically developed countries, with a vast outlay of intellectual and economic resources. And so it happens that while the people of these countries are loaded with heavy burdens, other countries as a result are deprived of the collaboration they need in order to make economic and social progress.

110. The production of arms is allegedly justified on the grounds that in present-day conditions peace cannot be preserved without an equal balance of armaments. And so, if one country increases its armaments, others feel the need to do the same; and if one country is equipped with nuclear weapons, other countries must produce their own, equally destructive.

111. Consequently, people live in constant fear lest the storm that every moment threatens should break upon them with dreadful violence. And with good reason, for the arms of war are ready at hand.

Even though it is difficult to believe that anyone would deliberately take the responsibility for the appalling destruction and sorrow that war would bring in its train, it cannot be denied that the conflagration may be set off by some uncontrollable and unexpected chance. And one must bear in mind that even though the monstrous power of modern weapons acts as a deterrent, it is to be feared that the mere continuance of nuclear tests, undertaken with war in mind, will have fatal consequences for life on the earth.

112. Justice, then, right reason, and humanity urgently demand that the arms race should cease; that the stockpiles which exist in various countries should be reduced equally and simultaneously by the parties concerned; that nuclear weapons should be banned; and that finally a general agreement should be reached about progressive disarmament and an effective method of control. In the words of Pius XII, Our Predecessor of happy memory: The calamity of a world war, with the economic and social ruin and the moral excesses and dissolution that accompany it, must not be permitted to envelop the human race for a third time.[59]

113. All must realize that there is no hope of putting an end to the building up of armaments, nor of reducing the present stocks, nor still less of abolishing them altogether unless the process is complete and thorough and unless it proceeds from inner conviction: unless, that is, everyone sincerely cooperates to banish the fear and anxious expectation of war with which men are oppressed. If this is to come about, the fundamental principle on which our present peace depends must be replaced by another, which declares that the true and solid peace of nations consists not in equality of arms but in mutual trust alone. We believe that this can be brought to pass, and We consider that it is something which reason requires, that it is eminently desirable in itself, and that it will prove to be the source of many benefits.

114. In the first place, it is an objective demanded by reason. There can be, or at least there should be, no doubt that relations between states, as between individuals, should be regulated not by the force of arms but by the light of reason, by the rule, that is, of truth, of justice, and of active and sincere cooperation.

[59]Pius XII's radio broadcast on Christmas Eve, 1941, in *op. cit.,* p. 17; see Benedict XV's *adhortatio* to the rulers of peoples at war, August 1, 1917, in *AAS,* IX (1917), 418.

115. Secondly, We say that it is an objective earnestly to be desired in itself. Is there anyone who does not ardently yearn to see war banished, to see peace preserved and daily more firmly established?

116. And finally, it is an objective which will be a fruitful source of many benefits, for its advantages will be felt overywhere, by individuals, by families, by nations, by the whole human family. The warning of Pius XII still rings in Our ears: Nothing is lost by peace; everything may be lost by war.[60]

117. Since this is so, We, the Vicar on earth of Jesus Christ, Savior of the world and Author of peace, and as interpreter of the very profound longing of the entire human family, following the impulse of Our heart, seized by anxiety for the good of all, We feel it Our duty to beseech men, especially those who have the responsibility of public affairs, to spare no labor in order to ensure that world events follow a reasonable and humane course.

118. In the highest and most authoritative assemblies, let men give serious thought to the problem of a peaceful adjustment of relations between political communities on a world level, an adjustment founded on mutual trust, on sincerity in negotiations, on faithful fulfillment of obligations assumed. Let them study the problem until they find that point of agreement from which it will be possible to commence to go forward toward accords that will be sincere, lasting, and fruitful.

119. We, for Our part, will not cease to pray God to bless these labors so that they may lead to fruitful results.

In Liberty

120. One must also bear in mind that relations between states should be based on freedom, that is to say, that no country may unjustly oppress others or unduly meddle in their affairs. On the contrary, all should help to develop in others a sense of responsibility, a spirit of enterprise, and an earnest desire to be the first to promote their own advancement in every field.

[60]Pius XII's radio broadcast on August 24, 1939, in *AAS*, XXXI (1939), 334.

Progress of Economically Underdeveloped Countries

121. Because all men are joined together by reason of their common origin, their redemption by Christ, and their supernatural destiny, and are called to form one Christian family, We appealed in the encyclical *Mater et Magistra* to economically developed nations to come to the aid of those which were in the process of development.[61]

122. We are greatly consoled to see how widely that appeal has been favorably received; and We are confident that even more so in the future it will contribute to the end that the poorer countries, in as short a time as possible, will arrive at that degree of economic development which will enable every citizen to live in conditions in keeping with his human dignity.

123. But it is never sufficiently repeated that the cooperation to which reference has been made should be effected with the greatest respect for the liberty of the countries being developed, for these must realize that they are primarily responsible, and that they are the principal artisans in the promotion of their own economic development and social progress.

124. Our Predecessor Pius XII already proclaimed that in the field of a new order founded on moral principles, there is no room for violation of the freedom, integrity, and security of other nations, no matter what may be their territorial extension or their capacity for defense. It is inevitable that the powerful states, by reason of their greater potential and their power, should pave the way in the establishment of economic groups comprising not only themselves but also smaller and weaker states as well. It is nevertheless indispensable that in the interests of the common good they, as all others, should respect the rights of those smaller states to political freedom, to economic development, and to the adequate protection, in the case of conflicts between nations, of that neutrality which is theirs according to the natural as well as international law. In this way and in this way only will they be able to obtain a fitting share of the common good and assure the material and spiritual welfare of their people.[62]

125. It is vitally important, therefore, that the wealthier states, in

[61]In *op. cit.,* pp. 440–441.

[62]See Pius XII's radio broadcast on Christmas Eve, 1941, in *op. cit.,* pp. 16–17.

providing varied forms of assistance to the poorer, should respect the moral values and ethnic characteristics peculiar to each, and also that they should avoid any intention of political domination. If this be done, it will help much toward shaping a community of all nations, wherein each one, aware of its rights and duties, will have regard for the prosperity of all.[63]

Signs of the Times

126. Men are becoming more and more convinced that disputes which arise between states should not be resolved by recourse to arms, but rather by negotiation.

127. It is true that on historical grounds this conviction is based chiefly on the terrible destructive force of modern arms; and it is nourished by the horror aroused in the mind by the very thought of the cruel destruction and immense suffering which the use of those armaments would bring to the human family. For this reason it is hardly possible to imagine that in the atomic era war could be used as an instrument of justice.

128. Nevertheless, unfortunately, the law of fear still reigns among peoples, and it forces them to spend fabulous sums for armaments: not for aggression, they affirm—and there is no reason for not believing them—but to dissuade others from aggression.

129. There is reason to hope, however, that by meeting and negotiating, men may come to discover better the bonds that unite them together, deriving from the human nature which they have in common; and that they may also come to discover that one of the most profound requirements of their common nature is this: that between them and their respective peoples it is not fear which should reign but love, a love which tends to express itself in collaboration that is loyal, manifold in form, and productive of many benefits.

[63]John XXIII's Encyclical Letter *Mater et Magistra,* in *op. cit.,* p. 443.

Part IV

The Relationship of Men and of Political Communities With the World Community

Interdependence Between Political Communities

130. Recent progress in science and technology has profoundly affected human beings and influenced men to work together as one family. There has been a great increase in the circulation of goods, of ideas, and of persons from one country to another, so that relations have become closer between individuals, families, and intermediate associations belonging to different political communities and between the public authorities of those communities. At the same time the interdependence of national economics has grown deeper, one becoming progressively more closely related to the other, so that they become, as it were, integral parts of the one world economy. Likewise, the social progress, order, security, and peace of each country are necessarily connected with the social progress, order, security, and peace of all other countries.

131. At the present day no political community is able to pursue its own interests and develop itself in isolation, because the degree of its prosperity and development is a reflection and a component part of the degree of prosperity and development of all the other political communities.

Existing Public Authority Is Not Equal to Requirements of the Universal Common Good

132. The unity of the human family has always existed, because its members were human beings all equal by virtue of their natural dignity. Hence there will always exist the objective need to promote in sufficient measure the universal common good, that is, the common good of the entire human family.

133. In times past, one would be justified in feeling that the public authorities of the different political communities might be in a position to provide for the universal common good, either through normal diplomatic channels or through top-level meetings, by making use of juridical instruments such as conventions and treaties, for example: juridical instruments suggested by the natural law and regulated by the law of nations and international law.

134. As a result of the far-reaching changes which have taken place in relations within the human community, the universal common good gives rise to problems that are very grave, complex, and extremely urgent, especially as regards security and world peace. On the other hand, the public authorities of the individual nations—being placed as they are on a footing of equality one with the other—no matter how much they multiply their meetings or sharpen their wits in efforts to draw up new juridical instruments, are no longer capable of facing the task of finding an adequate solution to the problems mentioned above. And this is not because of a lack of good will or of a spirit of enterprise, but because their authority lacks suitable force.

135. It can be said, therefore, that at this historical moment the present system of organization and the way its principle of authority operates on a world basis no longer correspond to the objective requirements of the universal common good.

Relations Between the Common Good and Public Authority in Historical Context

136. There exists an intrinsic connection between the common good on the one hand and the structure and function of public authority on the other. The moral order, which needs public authority in order to promote the common good in civil society, requires also that the authority be effective in attaining that end. This demands that the organs through which the authority is formed, becomes operative, and pursues its ends must be composed and act in such a manner as to be capable of furthering the common good by ways and means which correspond to the developing situation.

137. Today the universal common good poses problems of worldwide dimensions which cannot be adequately tackled or solved except by the efforts of public authorities endowed with a wideness of powers, structure, and means of the same proportions, that is, of public authorities which are in a position to operate in an effective manner on a worldwide basis. The moral order itself, therefore, demands that such a form of public authority be established.

Public Authority Instituted by Common Consent and Not Imposed by Force

138. A public authority having worldwide power and endowed with the proper means for the efficacious pursuit of its objective, which is the universal common good in concrete form, must be set up by common accord and not imposed by force. The reason is that such an authority must be in a position to operate effectively; yet at the same time its action must be inspired by sincere and real impartiality. In other words, it must be an action aimed at satisfying the objective requirements of the universal common good. The difficulty is that there would be reason to fear that a supranational or worldwide public authority, imposed by force by the more powerful political communities, might be or might become an instrument of one-sided interests; and even should this not happen, it would be difficult for it to avoid all suspicion of partiality in its actions, and this would take away from the efficaciousness of its activity. Even though there may be pronounced differences between political communities as regards the degree of their economic development and their military power, they are all very sensitive as regards their juridical equality and their moral dignity. For that reason, they are right in not easily yielding in obedience to an authority imposed by force, or to an authority in whose creation they had no part, or to which they themselves did not decide to submit by conscious and free choice.

The Universal Common Good and Personal Rights

139. Like the common good of individual political communities, so too the universal common good cannot be determined except by having regard to the human person. Therefore, the public authority of the world community too must have as its fundamental objective the recognition, respect, safeguarding, and promotion of the rights of the human person; this can be done by direct action when required, or by creating on a world scale an environment in which the public authorities of the individual political communities can more easily carry out their specific functions.

The Principle of Subsidiarity

140. Just as within each political community the relations between individuals, families, intermediate associations, and public authority are governed by the principle of subsidiarity, so too the relations between the public authority of each political community and the public authority of the world community must be regulated by the light of the same principle. This means that the public authority of the world community must tackle and solve problems of an economic, social, political, or cultural character which are posed by the universal common good. For because of the vastness, complexity, and urgency of those problems, the public authorities of the individual states are not in a position to tackle them with any hope of resolving them satisfactorily.

141. The public authority of the world community is not intended to limit the sphere of action of the public authority of the individual political community, much less to take its place. On the contrary, its purpose is to create on a world basis an environment in which the public authorities of each political community, its citizens, and its intermediate associations can carry out their tasks, fulfill their duties, and exercise their rights with greater security.[64]

Modern Developments

142. As is known, the United Nations Organization (UN) was established on June 26, 1945, and to it there were subsequently added intergovernmental agencies with extensive international tasks in the economic, social, cultural, educational, and health fields. The United Nations Organization had as its essential purpose the maintenance and consolidation of peace between peoples, fostering between them friendly relations based on the principles of equality, mutual respect, and varied forms of cooperation in every sector of human society.

[64]See Pius XII's allocution to the youth of Catholic Action from the dioceses of Italy gathered in Rome, September 12, 1948, in *AAS*, XL (1948), 412.

143. An act of the highest importance performed by the United Nations Organization was the Universal Declaration of the Rights of Man, approved in the General Assembly of December 10, 1948. In the preamble of that Declaration, the recognition of and respect for those rights and respective liberties is proclaimed as an ideal to be pursued by all peoples and all countries.

144. Some objections and reservations were raised regarding certain points in the Declaration. There is no doubt, however, that the document represents an important step on the path toward the juridical-political organization of the world community. For in it, in most solemn form, the dignity of a person is acknowledged to all human beings; and as a consequence there is proclaimed, as a fundamental right, the right of free movement in the search for truth and in the attainment of moral good and of justice, and also the right to a dignified life, while other rights connected with those mentioned are likewise proclaimed.

145. It is Our earnest wish that the United Nations Organization, in its structure and in its means, may become ever more equal to the magnitude and nobility of its tasks. May the day soon come when every human being will find therein an effective safeguard for the rights which derive directly from his dignity as a person and which are therefore universal, inviolate, and inalienable rights. This is all the more to be hoped for since all human beings, as they take an ever more active part in the public life of their own political communities, are showing an increasing interest in the affairs of all peoples, and are becoming more consciously aware that they are living members of the universal family of mankind.

Part V

Pastoral Exhortations

The Duty of Taking Part in Public Life

146. Once again We deem it opportune to remind Our children of their duty to take an active part in public life, and to contribute toward the attainment of the common good of the entire human family as well as to that of their own political community. Men should endeavor, therefore, in the light of the faith and with the strength of love, to ensure that the various institutions—whether economic, social, cultural, or political in purpose—will be such as not to create obstacles but rather to facilitate the task of improving themselves in the natural order as well as in the supernatural.

Scientific Competence, Technical Capacity, and Professional Experience

147. Nevertheless, in order to imbue civilization with sound principles and enliven it with the spirit of the Gospel, it is not enough to be illumined with the gift of faith and enkindled with the desire of forwarding a good cause. For this end it is necessary to take an active part in the various organizations and influence them from within.

148. But since our present age is one of outstanding scientific and technical progress and excellence, one will not be able to enter these organizations and work effectively from within unless he is scientifically competent, technically capable, and skilled in the practice of his own profession.

Action, the Outcome of Scientific-Technical-Professional Skill and of Spiritual Values

149. We desire to call attention to the fact that scientific competence, technical capacity, and professional experience, although necessary, are not of themselves sufficient to elevate the relationships of society to an order that is genuinely human, that is, to an order whose foundation is truth, whose measure and objective is justice, whose driving force is love, and whose method of attainment is freedom.

150. For this end it is certainly necessary that human beings carry on their own temporal activities in accordance with the laws governing them and following the methods corresponding to their nature. But at the same time it is also necessary that they should carry on those activities as acts within the moral order—therefore, as the exercise or vindication of a right, as the fulfillment of a duty or the performance of a service, as a positive answer to the providential design of God directed to our salvation. In other words, it is necessary that human beings, in the intimacy of their own consciences, should so live and act in their temporal lives as to create a synthesis between scientific, technical, and professional elements on the one hand and spiritual values on the other.

Reconciling of Faith and Action

151. It is no less clear that today in traditionally Christian nations secular institutions, although demonstrating a high degree of scientific and technical perfection and efficiency in achieving their respective ends, not infrequently are but slightly affected by Christian motivation or inspiration.

152. It is beyond question that in the creation of those institutions many contributed and continue to contribute who were believed to be and who consider themselves Christians; and without doubt, in part at least, they were and are. How does one explain this? It is Our opinion that the explanation is to be found in an inconsistency in their minds between religious belief and their action in the temporal sphere. It is necessary, therefore, that their interior unity be re-established, and that in their temporal activity faith should be present as a beacon to give light, and charity as a force to give life.

Education of the Whole Man

153. It is Our opinion, too, that the above-mentioned inconsistency between the religious faith in those who believe and their activities in the temporal sphere results—in great part if not entirely —from the lack of a solid Christian education. Indeed, it happens in many quarters and too often that there is no proportion between scientific training and religious instruction: the former continues and is extended until it reaches higher degrees, while the latter remains at an elementary level. It is indispensable, therefore, that in the training of youth, education should be complete and without interruption: namely, that in the minds of the young, religious values should be cultivated and the moral conscience refined in a manner to keep pace with the continuous and ever more abundant assimilation of scientific and technical knowledge. And it is indispensable too that they be instructed regarding the proper way to carry out their actual tasks.[65]

Constant Endeavor

154. We deem it opportune to point out how difficult it is to understand clearly the relation between the objective requirements of justice and concrete situations, namely, to perceive the degrees and forms in which doctrinal principles and directives ought to be applied to reality.

155. And in our day, when everyone should be striving to further the common good, the discernment of those degrees and forms is all the more difficult because of the dynamic course of events. Accordingly, since each day we must endeavor to see how social reality can be brought more into line with objective justice, Our sons should not think of ceasing from the effort or of resting by the wayside.

156. In fact, all human beings ought rather to reckon that what has been accomplished is but little in comparison with what remains to be done; because organs of production, trade unions, associations, professional organizations, insurance systems, legal systems, political regimes, institutions for cultural, health, recreational, or athletic purposes—these must all be adjusted to the era of the atom and of the conquest of space, an era which the human family has already entered, wherein it has commenced its new advance toward limitless horizons.

Relations Between Catholics and Non-Catholics in Social and Economic Affairs

157. The doctrinal principles outlined in this document derive from or are suggested by requirements inherent in human nature itself, and are for the most part dictates of the natural law. They

[65]See John XXIII's encyclical letter *Mater et Magistra*, in *op. cit.*, p. 454.

provide Catholics, therefore, with a vast field in which they can meet
and come to an understanding both with Christians separated from
this Apostolic See and also with human beings who are not enlightened by faith in Jesus Christ but who are endowed with the light of
reason and with a natural and operative honesty. On such occasions,
those who profess Catholicism must take special care to be consistent
and not compromise in matters wherein the integrity of religion or
morals would suffer harm. Likewise, in their conduct they should
weigh the opinions of others with fitting courtesy and not measure
everything in the light of their own interests. They should be prepared to join sincerely in doing whatever is naturally good or conducive to good.[66]

158. Moreover, one must never confuse error and the person who
errs, not even when there is question of error or inadequate knowledge of truth in the moral or religious field. The person who errs is
always and above all a human being, and he retains in every case his
dignity as a human person; and he must be always regarded and
treated in accordance with that lofty dignity. Besides, in every human
being there is a need that is congenital to his nature and never becomes extinguished, compelling him to break through the web of
error and open his mind to the knowledge of truth. And God will
never fail to act on his interior being, with the result that a person
who at a given moment of his life lacked the clarity of faith or even
adhered to erroneous doctrines can at a future date learn and believe
the truth. Meetings and agreements, in the various sectors of daily
life, between believers and those who do not believe or believe insufficiently because they adhere to error, can be occasions for discovering
truth and paying homage to it.

159. It must be borne in mind, furthermore, that neither can
false philosophical teachings regarding the nature, origin, and destiny
of the universe and of man be identified with historical movements
that have economic, social, cultural, or political ends, not even when
these movements have originated from those teachings and have
drawn and still draw inspiration therefrom. For these teachings, once
they are drawn up and defined, remain always the same, while the
movements, working on historical situations in constant evolution,
cannot but be influenced by these latter and cannot avoid, therefore,
being subject to changes, even of a profound nature. Besides, who can

[66]See *ibid.*, p. 456.

deny that those movements, insofar as they conform to the dictates of right reason and are interpreters of the lawful aspirations of the human person, contain elements that are positive and deserving of approval?

160. It can happen, then, that a drawing nearer together or a meeting for the attainment of some practical end, which was formerly deemed inopportune or unproductive, might now or in the future be considered opportune and useful. But to decide whether this moment has arrived, and also to lay down the ways and degrees in which work in common might be possible for the achievement of economic, social, cultural, and political ends which are honorable and useful—these are the problems which can only be solved with the virtue of prudence, which is the guiding light of the virtues that regulate the moral life, both individual and social. Therefore, so far as Catholics are concerned, this decision rests primarily with those who live and work in the specific sectors of human society in which those problems arise, always, however, in accordance with the principles of the natural law, with the social teaching of the Church, and with the directives of ecclesiastical authority. For it must not be forgotten that the Church has the right and the duty not only to safeguard the principles of ethics and religion but also to intervene authoritatively with her children in the temporal sphere when there is a question of judging about the application of those principles to concrete cases.[67]

Little by Little

161. There are some souls particularly endowed with generosity who, on finding situations where the requirements of justice are not satisfied or not satisfied in full, feel enkindled with the desire to change the state of things, as if they wished to have recourse to something like a revolution.

162. It must be borne in mind that to proceed gradually is the law of life in all its expressions; therefore, in human institutions, too,

[67]See *ibid.*; Leo XIII's encyclical letter *Immortale Dei*, in *op. cit.*, p. 128; Pius XI's encyclical letter *Ubi arcano*, in *AAS*, XIV (1922), 698; and Pius XII's allocution to delegates of the International Union of Catholic Women's Leagues gathered in Rome for a joint convention, September 11, 1947, in *AAS*, XXXIX (1947), 486.

it is not possible to renovate the better except by working from within them, gradually. Pius XII proclaimed: Salvation and justice are not to be found in revolution, but in evolution through concord. Violence has always achieved only destruction, not construction; the kindling of passions, not their pacification; the accumulation of hate and ruin, not the reconciliation of the contending parties. And it has reduced men and parties to the difficult task of rebuilding, after sad experience, on the ruins of discord.[68]

An Immense Task

163. There is an immense task incumbent on all men of good will, namely, the task of restoring the relations of the human family in truth, in justice, in love, and in freedom: the relations between individual human beings; between citizens and their respective political communities; between political communities themselves; between individuals, families, intermediate associations, and political communities on the one hand and the world community on the other. This is a most exalted task, for it is the task of bringing about true peace in the order established by God.

164. Admittedly, those who are endeavoring to restore the relations of social life according to the criteria mentioned above are not many; to them We express Our paternal appreciation, and We earnestly invite them to persevere in their work with ever greater zeal. And We are comforted by the hope that their number will increase, especially among Christian believers. For it is an imperative of duty; it is a requirement of love. Every believer in this world of ours must be a spark of light, a center of love, a vivifying leaven amidst his fellow men: and he will be this all the more perfectly the more closely he lives in communion with God in the intimacy of his own soul.

165. In fact, there can be no peace between men unless there is peace within each of them, unless, that is, each one builds up within himself the order wished by God. Hence St. Augustine asks: Does your soul desire to overcome your lower inclinations? Let it be subject to Him Who is on high, and it will conquer the lower self; there

[68]See Pius XII's allocution to workers from the dioceses of Italy gathered in Rome on the Feast of Pentecost, June 13, 1943, in *AAS*, XXXV (1943), 175.

will be peace in you, true, secure and well-ordered peace. In what does that order consist? God commands the soul; the soul commands the body; and there is nothing more orderly than this.[69]

The Prince of Peace

166. These words of Ours, which We have wished to dedicate to the problems which so beset the human family today and on the just solution of which the ordered progress of society depends, are dictated by a profound aspiration which We know is shared by all men of good will: the consolidation of peace in the world.

167. As the humble and unworthy Vicar of Him Whom the prophet announced as the Prince of peace,[70] We have the duty to expend all Our energies in an effort to protect and strengthen this gift. However, peace will be but an empty-sounding word unless it is founded on the order which this present encyclical has outlined in confident hope: an order founded on truth, built according to justice, vivified and integrated by charity, and put into practice in freedom.

168. This is such a noble and elevated task that human resources, even though inspired by the most praiseworthy good will, cannot bring it to realization alone. In order that human society may reflect as faithfully as possible the Kingdom of God, help from on high is necessary.

169. For this reason, during these sacred days Our supplication is raised with greater fervor toward Him Who by His painful passion and death overcame sin—the root of discord and the source of sorrows and inequalities—and by His blood reconciled mankind to the eternal Father; for He Himself is our peace, He it is that has made both one. . . . And coming He announced the good tidings of peace to you who were afar off, and of peace to those who were near.[71]

170. And in the Liturgy of these days we hear the announcement: Our Lord Jesus Christ, after His resurrection, stood in the midst of His disciples and said, "Peace be to you," alleluia: the disciples re-

[69]*Miscellanea Augustiniana* . . . , St. Augustine's *Sermones post Maurinos reperti*, Rome, 1930, p. 633.

[70]See Is 9:6.

[71]Eph 2:14–17.

joiced seeing the Lord.[72] He leaves us peace, He brings us peace: Peace I leave with you, my peace I give to you; not as the world gives do I give to you.[73]

171. This is the peace which We implore of Him with the ardent yearning of Our prayer. May He banish from the hearts of men whatever might endanger peace; may He transform them into witnesses of truth, justice, and brotherly love. May He enlighten the rulers of peoples so that in addition to their solicitude for the proper welfare of their citizens, they may guarantee and defend the great gift of peace. Finally, may Christ enkindle the wills of all, so that they may overcome the barriers that divide, cherish the bonds of mutual charity, understand others, and pardon those who have done them wrong. By virtue of His action, may all peoples of the earth become as brothers, and may the most longed-for peace blossom forth and reign always between them.

172. As a pledge of this peace, and with the ardent wish that it may shine forth on the flocks entrusted to your care, especially for the benefit of those who are most lowly and in the greatest need of help and defense, We affectionately impart to you, venerable brothers, to the priests both secular and religious, to the religious men and women, and to all the Christian faithful, particularly to those who make every effort to put these exhortations of Ours into practice, Our apostolic blessing in propitiation of heavenly favors. Finally, for all men of good will, to whom this encyclical letter is also addressed, We implore from Almighty God health and prosperity.

173. Given at Rome at St. Peter's on Holy Thursday, the eleventh day of April, in the year 1963, the fifth of Our Pontificate.

JOHN XXIII, POPE

[72]Responsory at Matins on the Friday after Easter.
[73]Jn 14:27.

Index

251